Contents

Introduction

Children learn through talk. This is well documented and backed up by all who work in this field. Research into how children learn stresses the fundamental importance of talk in the learning process. It is not simply a good, sociable thing to do, but it is an effective means of developing children's learning. Indeed there is now evidence that indicates a positive relationship between talk and academic achievement.

It is through speech that children begin to formulate and organise their thoughts and ideas. The articulation of these ideas helps to make children's thinking explicit. Through talk, children are not merely conveying ideas but are clarifying their thinking by explaining these ideas to others. During the act of explaining, contrary to what might be anticipated, the main beneficiary is the child who is articulating their thoughts, rather than the listener.

It is accepted by many that talk is a way of developing understanding, enabling children to make links between new experiences and what is already known, to reshape current knowledge in the light of new ideas.

The approach undertaken in this book emphasises the inextricable link between speaking and listening. For children to be effective listeners they need opportunities to reply, participate and take action. For children to talk in a meaningful way they need to know that others are actively listening. Based on these premises, discussion and decision making are central to the activities in this book.

The activities support the objectives for Speaking and listening in the National Curriculum, the Talking and listening outcomes of the Scottish English language 5–14 guidelines, and the objectives in Teaching Speaking and listening in Key Stages 1 and 2 (QCA, 1999). The book has been designed to help teachers to undertake speaking and listening activities with their pupils within appropriate contexts. Many of these contexts are linked to the National Curriculum history, geography and science programmes and to the Scottish environmental studies 5–14 guidelines.

▌ Importance of context

Until recently much of the available material related to the development of speaking and listening has involved children working their way through decontextualised speaking and listening exercises. These exercises are unrelated to each other, do not enhance any other aspect of their work and encourage little in the way of commitment from the children.

Although placed in the English curriculum, it is widely recognised by teachers and others that speaking and listening are essential aspects of learning in all areas of the curriculum. The contexts used for the speaking and listening activities in this book are linked with topics currently undertaken in schools in relation to the National Curriculum for history, geography and science, the Scottish environmental studies 5–14 guidelines and the National Literacy Strategy *Framework for Teaching*.

Setting the speaking and listening activities within a context:

- provides a purpose for children's talk
- enables children to use talk as a tool for learning across the curriculum
- extends children's knowledge and understanding in other curricular areas
- enhances children's participation in the speaking and listening activities.

▮ Meeting teachers' needs

This book aims to increase teachers' confidence in undertaking this often neglected area of the curriculum by addressing their concerns in the following ways:

Providing ideas

Many teachers acknowledge that the demands on them are such that it is not always possible to plan good speaking and listening activities, or that they sometimes run out of fresh ideas. This book aims to provide well-structured, clearly outlined activities for teachers, the basic ideas of which can be transferred to other contexts.

Identifying teaching content

There has been a tendency to assume that because speaking and listening are naturally occurring phenomena for most children, that skills will continue to develop through the provision of speaking and listening activities alone. This book recognises key skills which children need to be taught in order to become adept in a range of speaking and listening situations. Within each activity teaching points are identified and suggestions are made in relation to how these points might be modelled and developed with the children.

Assessment

It is commonly accepted that speaking and listening, particularly when related to group discussion, are difficult areas to assess. In this book there is advice about what to assess and how to assess in an area where there may be little hard evidence for assessment.

Managing groups

Guidance regarding the organisation and management of activities has been included to enable the smooth implementation of speaking and listening activities in the classroom. Teachers' concerns about noise, safety, behaviour and so on can act as a barrier in undertaking speaking and listening activities. This book aims to increase teacher confidence by providing suggestions about managing groups that will ensure that children remain focused and actively involved in the activities.

Time

This book has also been written in response to teachers who view time as a barrier to implementing speaking and listening activities, by integrating this as a way of learning in history, geography and science/environmental studies.

▌ Using the activities

The activities have been devised to allow teachers the freedom to use them either as a part of their English programmes or as part of their history, geography and science programmes. The latter enables activities to be conducted as a natural part of ongoing work in these areas of the curriculum; so children's learning in geography, for example, will be reinforced by their learning in English language.

Some teachers may wish to use these activities as part of the Literacy Hour or Language Time. If this is the case, the four or so activities for each topic will provide some coherence for children's learning, particularly if they are undertaken within a condensed period of time.

Transfer to other topics

Many of the activities have been designed with flexibility in mind, and without too much difficulty can be transferred to other topics. For example, if teachers are studying the Second World War with their classes they may find that many of the activities outlined in 'The 1960s' (see pages 29–43) need only minor adjustments to make them relevant to the 1940s. Some units have been written with a more general approach, for example the 'Exploration and discovery' activities (see pages 59–72) could be applied to many different time eras.

Class or group work

The optimum number of children who can work together in many of the activities is often no more than four. This does not necessarily mean that only four children will undertake the task. Teachers may wish to break the class into groups of four and have all children working on the same task simultaneously. Or they may prefer to have only four children working on the task at any one time but with the task being staggered throughout the week, so that every child experiences it at some point. On some occasions it may be decided that not every child need undertake every task. Indeed the oral presentation sessions may become counterproductive if every group presents its findings to the rest of the class!

Classroom techniques

Encouraging children to speak and listen effectively entails more than simply providing a context and associated activities for them. Developing children's skills in speaking and listening requires teachers to consider the classroom techniques that will enhance these skills. The following suggestions will be useful to teachers wishing to instigate and develop good practices in speaking and listening in the classroom.

▌Speaking

Speaking effectively in different situations involves children in speaking informally during group or paired discussions as well as addressing an audience in a formal manner. Both aspects of speaking require children to develop different skills, and teachers to introduce different techniques.

Oral presentations

Addressing an audience is said to be one of the most commonly feared experiences for many adults. It is therefore very important that children are offered much support in undertaking oral presentations. Perhaps the most crucial part of undertaking any presentation is having time to plan, prepare and rehearse beforehand. The speaking activities in this book are backed up by materials to help children plan and prepare and it is crucial that teachers allow sufficient time for these as well as giving a quiet space for children to rehearse.

Using notes

Children need help in writing notes rather than full scripts, but perhaps it is best to start by writing full scripts, then using headings, bullet points, underlining and so on to highlight the salient points. This is best taught as and when children require this help, for example in preparation for real or mock interviews, debates and presentations. Allowing children to refer to their notes (rather than reading directly from them) will boost their confidence. This is a skill that improves only with practice and praise.

Meeting the audience's needs

It is important that children begin to tailor their talk to suit different audiences in different situations, for example formal debates, presentations and interviews. They should also be encouraged to think about ways of interesting and involving their audiences. Asking the audience to predict, guess or vote, for example, often increases involvement and interest.

A talk to peers who have also been studying the topic on which the talk is based may include very specific terminology related to the topic, whereas an audience which does not have this background knowledge would need certain terms explained. The pace for an audience of infants would be different from an adult audience as would the number and types of visual aids. Consideration of the needs of the audience might be helped by the use of photocopiable page 17 on occasion.

Using visual aids

The use of visual aids in formal presentations always helps to motivate both the presenters and the audience and again children will need some training as to how to operate overhead projectors and so on. As with preparing notes, children will benefit most from any training that takes place just prior to their own presentation.

Giving children limits

Many children might need help here and if planning presentations is new to them they may find comfort in being given time limits and tight conditions on any presentation, for example *you must use the overhead projector but you can use no more than three visual aids.*

When children are new to presenting they should be asked to speak for very short periods of time and this should be increased until children are deciding upon the most appropriate time for their own presentations.

Use of standard English

The use of standard English is often considered essential for many formal speaking activities. However, the audience's needs and/or the subject matter may demand the use of dialects.

Again children should be encouraged to consider the most appropriate form (or combination of forms) to use for each speaking activity.

Use of appropriate language features

The ability to choose and use appropriate language features (for example, syntax, vocabulary, style of address, use of persuasive phrases, and so on) when children are speaking in different situations needs to be developed over time.

▌Listening

Passive listening – that is, listening that demands little or no real response – will do little to motivate or inspire children and it could be said that education in the past demanded too much of children in this way. Listeners need to feel some connection with the speaker(s) if they are to gain from the experience. This holds true whether the listening is undertaken as part of a group discussion or during a presentation.

Activities in this book have been devised to maximise the responses from audiences and so make listening an active experience whereby children listen in order to modify their point of view, to reflect on their own use of language as well of that of others, or to develop their ideas.

Active audiences

As indicated in the Speaking section above, speakers should try to involve the audience in some way to maintain interest. The audience should also feel free to take notes on any aspect of a presentation over and above the tasks that the speaker has set. Children could be issued with personal note pads for such a purpose in order to give listening a higher status. Before any presentations the note pad could be used to note any task that the speaker has set as well as noting any responses during the presentation. During group discussions, when children do not want to interrupt a speaker, they might be encouraged to use their note pad to note quickly a point that they may want to raise later.

Eye contact

During any discussion or presentation, children should be made aware of the effect that eye contact can have on the speaker and other listeners. Appropriate eye contact should be highlighted, or more importantly, modelled by the teacher during discussions or presentations. Note that good eye contact is probably more appropriate during presentations than during group discussions. Indeed looking too closely at a person when they are thinking on their feet can be a little off-putting. More often than not the group discussions will involve some physical resources (for example, cards to be sorted in some way) which will demand that eyes are kept on these while the discussion continues.

Body language

Good audience behaviour during a presentation sometimes needs to be taught directly to children. Vigorous head shaking or 'making faces' can be very off-putting to a presenter and should be discouraged! Even when the listeners are in agreement with what is being said they should normally refrain from head nodding, cheering, clapping or giving the thumbs-up sign or similar. Instead they should note the things with which they particularly agree and refer to these points after the presentation.

Much of this applies to body language during group discussions. Waiting until people have finished making their point before agreeing, disagreeing or changing the direction of the talk is a skill that takes some people a lifetime to develop. We should not be encouraging children to take turns during a group discussion; that would stifle the making of meaning. However, we can train children to be aware of certain conventions of good group discussion. These are outlined overleaf.

Allowing others to talk

Encouraging children to listen more to others in a group discussion is not easy and a few children simply want to talk. There are a few tricks to help curb this instinct in some children, for example asking these children to take a red counter every time they speak and putting a limit on the number to be collected. These same children might also be asked to take a green counter when they ask a question or an opinion of another child; they should be encouraged to collect as many of these as they can. These rather false devices should be used only at the training stage of the few children that need them, but they can be an effective way of encouraging children to listen a little more thoughtfully.

Reading the body language of others

Noticing when someone else wants to speak by reading their body language can be modelled by the teacher during discussions that she is involved in, simply saying something like, *Debbie, I see that you are looking thoughtful. Do you want to add anything here?* or *You look as though you don't agree, Vikram. Tell us what you think.*

Although most group discussions will not require a chairperson it might be worthwhile asking children who find it hard to listen to others to chair discussions. They will need to be trained to scan the talkers to notice facial expressions and other body movements, like leaning forward, which may denote a desire to participate. When all else fails, children should be given, or should devise for themselves, a signal to others that they want to be heard. This signal could be a raised forefinger or the taking of a counter from the middle of the table. However, it should be seen as undesirable to have to resort to these means too often. Children should be made aware that if they have to signal too often then the group members are not 'listening with their eyes'.

▌ Group discussion

Encouraging children to speak effectively in groups is not as easy as it sounds. Most people might think that since children talk readily to one another in the playground that they will have no difficulty in discussing topics in groups. Experienced teachers who have been met with silence or bewildered looks after presenting topics to children know that this is far from the truth. The following recommendations will help teachers to set up effective group discussions.

Designing children's tasks

Perhaps one of the trickiest aspects of teaching group discussion relates to the planning of children's tasks. Tasks should be tightly focused and children normally respond well when they are stepped in some way.

Teachers may find the following list helpful when thinking about how to adapt or design tasks that will help children to develop their discussion skills:

- Add to/amend/remove/select items from a given list.
- Group statements about something under given headings.
- Categorise and devise headings for statements, objects and so on.
- Prioritise statements, steps, procedures and so on according to given criteria.
- Note pros/cons of given features of objects, items and so on (for example, the safety, appeal, texture, colour of babies' toys).
- Sort statements into *agree/disagree/can't decide* or *true/false*.
- Give precise criteria for children to adhere to, for example *captions should have no more than six words*.
- Compare two things under given headings.
- Choose from options and justify choices.
- Convert from one form to another, for example text to map, diagram to 3-D model, text to illustration.
- Order items, procedures, events and so on according to given or agreed criteria.

Group composition

An effective group composition is necessary if children are to be encouraged to participate equally. Given that speaking and listening takes place across the whole curriculum and that children are grouped according to attainment levels for some subjects but not for others, it is important to be clear about the different reasons for grouping in speaking and listening.

Current thinking suggests that children should be grouped according to their confidence levels. This organisation may therefore involve mixed attainment groups and would mean asking shy children to work together in their groups and confident children to work in their groups. It is true that some shy children may be reluctant to talk even to one another but if asked to at first work in pairs they might eventually have a chance to build up their confidence. The problems associated with grouping very confident children together are perhaps more glaring! They may be noisy at first but will soon learn that they cannot easily dominate children who are of a similar level of confidence to themselves. Again paired work might be the quieter option here to start with.

Bilingual children might also benefit from speaking and listening with those whom they feel comfortable with and should be free to speak in their first language or English.

Some children may feel more confident when talking in single gender groups, particularly if the subject matter is sensitive.

On many occasions the purpose and nature of the activity will determine the number of children in the group. For example, if children are talking while working on the computer, then perhaps talking in pairs, or trios, would be appropriate. Unless otherwise stated, the activities in this book have been designed with groups of four children in mind. This appears to be the optimum number for children to speak and listen comfortably to one another and to benefit from pooling ideas.

Differentiation

All children, regardless of attainment levels, need time to talk to help them clarify their thinking. The tasks in this book have been devised with extensions and simplifications to help teachers to differentiate them to suit the needs of the children in their class. You will be the best judge as to what needs to be adapted for your pupils.

Teacher's role

In the activities in this book, the teacher, by and large, should not be present during group discussion, unless otherwise indicated. Indeed guidance given in the Programme of Study for the strand 'Talking in groups' at Level D in the Scottish English language 5–14 guidelines indicates that *Groups should now be able to work independently much of the time, discussing tasks and how to deal with them.*

It will be obvious to most teachers that the reason we are urging teachers not to be present during a group discussion is that the nature of that discussion will be substantially different with you there. There are two main reasons for this. First, no matter how much we try it is difficult for many of us to keep our contributions to a minimum and to take a back seat during group discussions with children. Indeed often what we think has been a good discussion has consisted of a question and answer session with the children. You will not need to ask who was asking the questions – tape yourself sometime and listen! Second, in spite of the excellent ethos you may have created in the classroom, children are still likely to acquiesce to you and seek your approval or be less willing to take risks with their ideas if you are present during their discussion. This will clearly affect the potential of the group discussion in developing learning through talk.

Some teachers may find it difficult to convince themselves to relinquish control of the discussion to a great extent. This may particularly be the case with children who are considered to have behavioural difficulties. Research and experience have shown us that these children benefit substantially from this type of learning. Reasons for this are associated with the following: children are provided with more variety in the types of activities they are given; esteem is often raised as children feel they have something to contribute to the group; children are committed to the activity and do not want to let the group down. Clearly group discussion activities will need to be carefully planned for many children who find it difficult to collaborate with others. It is certainly the case that if teachers do not provide opportunities for children to work together in groups they will continue to experience difficulties with this!

When you might intervene and how

Clearly there will be times when, from your monitoring of participation and progress, sensitive intervention will be judged to be necessary. This might include times when:

- some children are dominating
- some children are not participating
- ideas are being misunderstood
- reassurance is required
- language usage needs to be extended.

Before intervening in a group discussion, watch and listen for an opportune time to break in without interrupting a child when he or she is speaking. Position yourself beside the group and try to gain eye contact with all of the children. This will enable your contributions, whether verbal or non-verbal, to be regarded as an intrinsic part of the group process.

Hints on participating with a group

At some point in certain activities we have suggested that you participate with the group, for example to model a particular skill, explain an idea, share some information or listen to the group's ideas. For you to do this and still encourage children to have ownership of the discussion the following strategies may be effective:

- Encourage children to say more rather than saying it for them.
- Ask more open questions.
- Increase the length of time you give children to respond after asking a question, in order to give them time to think about their response. This is likely to encourage greater participation and fuller contributions.
- Use alternatives to questions, such as statements, constructive comments and encouraging gestures.
- Listen more carefully and for longer periods.

Group techniques

The following techniques are useful generally in the development of group discussion. To help you to see how the application of these techniques might look, an activity which incorporates each of the techniques has been indicated.

	How to	Useful for	Activity
Brainstorming	Brainstorming allows for *all* ideas related to the topic or issue to be voiced and written down. Only after the ideas have been exhausted does the sifting process begin in which impractical or impossible ideas are eliminated. Thereafter ideas can be grouped into areas for investigation.	Encouraging less confident children; starting off a topic; generating new ideas; pooling new and old ideas; reordering thinking.	'Leave the car – take the bus', page 74
Snowballing	Snowballing involves children working in pairs in order to develop some initial ideas. After a specified time each pair is asked to join up with another pair either to develop a new consensus or to build their ideas into a combined response. The ideas at this stage can be shared with the class, or fours can become eights, repeating the sharing and distilling process, before children share their ideas with the rest of the class.	Generating and clarifying ideas; negotiating within increasingly larger groups; weaning children away from the security of the pair and small group towards speaking and listening in a larger forum.	'Different coastlines for different people', page 90
Envoying	In envoying the whole class usually works in groups on the same activity (although this technique can also work successfully if groups have been working on different aspects of a topic). After a specified length of time and once groups have completed that part of the activity, the children are asked to nominate a representative to act as an 'envoy'. The envoy from each group moves to a new group to summarise and explain their group's ideas and, where appropriate, gather at least one additional idea. Again, after a specified time, envoys return and report back to their own group. The group also report back to the envoy on ideas discussed while an envoy from another group was with them. This means each group will have gained some feedback from two other groups. The group then revises its initial ideas, in light of the feedback and fresh insight, and proceeds with the activity.	Questioning, reformulating and clarifying ideas; explaining ideas; collecting new ideas; encouraging active listening; building confidence in reporting back within smaller groups; providing an alternative to whole-class plenary sessions.	'What is a seed?', page 118
Jigsawing/ expert groups	As with envoying (see above), the whole class usually work in groups on the same activity. Jigsawing often places children into 'home' groups and 'expert' groups. To begin with, the children gather in home groups to talk about how to divide up the activity or topic between the group members. 'Expert' groups are then formed, comprising all the children who have been assigned the same issue or aspect of the topic. (For example, with a class of 30 children and a topic that can be divided into three key areas, there may be five home groups, each with two children representing each topic area. These pairs of children can then form into three expert groups, each with ten 'experts' in them.) The experts work collaboratively until they have completed their task. They then return to their home groups to explain their area of expertise to the others and to share their findings.	Enabling children to become 'expert' in an aspect of a particular topic; providing opportunities for them to work in different groupings; encouraging all children to contribute.	'Pedestrian precinct problem', page 81
Allocating roles/ taking notes	A chairperson or scribe is appointed by the group or the teacher. This may be helpful if the children in a group are not experienced in participating in group discussion, or if they are not used to working with each other. However, an effective group discussion is more likely when group members are able to contribute without any direction from others. Care should also be given when one member of the group has been nominated as scribe as this can result in their exclusion from the discussion. It is anticipated, therefore, that throughout the activities in the book that all group members make notes on a recording sheet. However, allocating this role to a dominant group member can help to refocus that child and enable increased participation by others in the group.	Keeping track of ideas; maintaining involvement; ensuring all group members have opportunities to contribute; redirecting a more dominant group member.	'1960s people', page 30

Clearly there is more to enabling children to participate in successful group discussions than using these techniques. Further guidance is offered within activities for the modelling of specific group discussion behaviours and the introduction of useful linguistic formulas. Reference should also be made to key techniques in the section on listening (see page 8), where advice is given on allowing others to talk, as well as on reading others' body language.

▌Drama

Drama has long been recognised as a medium for children to express their thoughts and emotions as well as being a tool for learning across the curriculum. The drama techniques outlined below can be used not only to promote children's verbal communication but to help them to organise and articulate their thinking about a wide variety of issues and to explore characters in greater depth, including their motives, feelings and actions. As children become more confident in the use of these techniques, teachers will be able to use them in a more flexible way with their classes, identifying opportunities in other curricular areas.

Most of the drama activities here do not require space larger than the average classroom. However, it might be worthwhile establishing routines for the movement of tables and chairs to create appropriate space for children to work effectively.

Like oral presentations, undertaking drama activities can cause some children to feel a little self-conscious at first. Sensitive teachers will be aware that these children might benefit from working first with a partner, then in a trio of children of similar personality. However, one of the advantages of drama is that it can often give children an opportunity to use the protection of role-play to move beyond the confines of their own experiences and feelings in order to express new thoughts and ideas.

	What is it?	Useful for	Activity
Hot-seating	One person is in role and is questioned by the class, or by a group, who are usually not in role. The responses should be consistent with the role. The person in the hot seat could be one of the children, the teacher or a visitor.	Enhancing role; exploring character and motivation; gaining further information about a character.	'Hot-seating Pasteur', page 132
Freeze frame	Also referred to as *tableaux*, the children select or are given a key moment and make a still picture scene based on it. These can be done on an individual basis, or can be linked as a sequence by movement, narration, music, poetry and so on. The still picture can be activated to encourage children to 'come to life' briefly, or individuals in the frame can be encouraged to speak their thoughts.	Introducing the idea of images; encouraging selectivity and economy of expression; promoting discussion about meanings behind actions.	'Dramatising the myth', page 49
Documentary	The children present information about a topic. This may include a variety of techniques – freeze frames, interviewing and so on.	Encouraging wider research and some measure of factual accuracy; enabling groups to contribute their own interests; raising awareness about different forms of presentation; informing other groups and audiences.	'News of the decade', page 32

	What is it?	Useful for	Activity
Communal voice	Many children are involved in voicing one character's speech. The children place themselves behind the character, who is generally silent, and together they speak the character's words.	Enabling many children to be involved; providing security by participating in a whole-group activity; creating atmosphere; helping children to read and speak with meaning and feeling; deepening understanding of character and so on.	'An explorer's thoughts', page 65
Thought-tracking	Children, in roles, are asked to speak aloud their private thoughts, feelings and reactions to situations and events.	Presenting a powerful image; creating tension; developing speech without acting out; deepening understanding of character.	'An explorer's thoughts', page 65
Meetings	The children come together, in role, in a meeting to present information, plan action, suggest strategies and solve problems. The role is usually a demonstration of an attitude or viewpoint. It can be linked to the jigsawing technique used in group discussion (see page 14).	Getting groups into role easily; allowing the possibility of expert roles; encouraging appropriate behaviour through the meeting structure.	'Pedestrian precinct problem', page 81
Role-play	Children take on the role of another character, real or imagined. Role-play can be set into many contexts and can be spontaneous or rehearsed. It is most effective when children have some experience or knowledge of the situations and characters being 'played'.	Enabling shyer children to participate (they don't have to be themselves!); gaining a different perspective on situations and characters; encouraging language appropriate to a particular situation, character or period.	'Different coastlines for different people', page 90
Conscience alley	Also referred to as *thought tunnel*, the class are formed into two lines between which a character can walk. As the character walks down the 'alley', the character's thoughts are spoken aloud as he or she passes each child. The character may be on their way to an event or may have a difficult decision to make. If the character is faced with a dilemma, then the children on one side of the 'alley' could outline thoughts associated with one perspective and the other side could outline thoughts associated with a different perspective.	Examining issues from more than one viewpoint; creating tension; deepening understanding of situations, events and characters.	'Fair trade', page 63
Mime	This can be undertaken individually or as a group, usually without speech. It can range from simple mimes – moving like clockwork toys, for example – to more precise and powerful uses of gesture, movement and expression.	Deepening understanding of character, phenomena and situations; examining the impressions given through gestures, movement, expressions; developing non-verbal communication.	'Dramatising the adventures', page 141

Speaking to different audiences

▌ Before planning what you will actually say you have to think about your audience. In your groups discuss each point and take notes.

Audience	Notes/resources
Average age? Does this matter?	
How long could they listen for?	
How quickly/slowly should we speak to keep their interest?	
Are there any words that might not be understood by this audience?	
What visual aids would be helpful to the audience? How many?	
How could we involve them (eg ask them to: listen for particular things; vote; ask questions at the end; predict something; guess something before telling them the answer)?	
Should we use standard English? Our own dialect? A mixture?	

Assessment

▌Objectives and assessment

Every activity in this book contains *assessment* points which are closely related to the *objectives* for the activity. The close relationship between these two elements ensures that there is a clear and appropriate focus for teaching, learning and the assessment of learning. The objectives are based on Key Stage 2 attainment target descriptors for Levels 3–5, but are broken down and made more specific in individual activities (Levels C–E, Talking and listening outcomes, English language 5–14 guidelines). Teachers can feel reassured that through undertaking assessment of activity objectives they will gain an overall picture of children's progress in meeting the targets for Speaking and listening at this stage.

▌Recording assessment

Teachers will be monitoring children's speaking and listening informally on an ongoing basis. However, there are times when it is useful for a more focused assessment of a particular aspect of speaking and listening to be undertaken. A range of recording sheets has been provided (see pages 23–8) to assist teachers and children in assessing progress in speaking and listening. In a busy classroom, teachers do not have time to undertake lengthy assessments. However, ticking off items on a checklist may not be time well spent in providing a picture of the child in some of the more complex aspects of speaking and listening. Key considerations in devising these sheets, therefore, have been that they are practical *and* useful to teachers and children. Some sheets can be used to assess more than one aspect of speaking and listening at the same time, while others are dedicated to one particular aspect. Teachers should select the recording sheet they will use in relation to the focus for assessment and the objectives of the activity.

▌Self and group assessment

Evidence of learning will not only be gained through teacher assessment. A great deal of valuable information can be gleaned from children undertaking constructive self and group assessment. Teachers should encourage children's reflection on their talk on an ongoing basis, linked to the objectives of the activity. Occasionally, children could be asked to complete a written self-assessment, similar to the example given on photocopiable page 23. If children are asked to write a self-assessment too frequently there is a danger that it either becomes seen as a chore, or it lacks substance. Either way it can work against the concept of children reflecting usefully on the effectiveness of their speaking and listening. The aspects included in the self-assessment example would also serve as a useful starting point for occasions when a discussion between the teacher and individual children is possible.

As well as individuals reflecting on their speaking and listening, teachers should encourage groups to review the success of group interaction in achieving the objectives. Some time should be built in for groups to undertake this reflection, normally at the end of an activity. This process should be undertaken whether the teacher is present or not. It may be useful to be present during the reflective discussion on occasions when the group, or individuals in the group, have been the focus for assessment by the teacher. The framework on photocopiable page 24 may aid the process of reflection and help children and teachers to identify subsequent steps in speaking and listening. It would be wise to provide children with a copy of this page to help to guide their discussion. However, caution is advised in the use of these questions, lest the discussion becomes routinised and unproductive.

Teachers should work with children to ensure that the group assessment is constructive and focuses on success and development and does not single out individuals for critical comment.

▌Assessing speaking

The assessment of speaking and listening presents many problems to the classroom teacher, not least because of the different purposes of more formal speaking activities and group discussion. Formal speaking offers children a means of systematically ordering and rehearsing their thoughts, while discussions provide children with a way of creating meaning with others, and this process is often rather messy and tentative. Given these fundamental differences, some teachers may find it best to assess the different types of speaking using different criteria. Photocopiable page 25 has therefore been provided for assessing different aspects of formal speaking (as in a debate, an interview or a presentation, for example).

It could be said that the assessment of formal speaking, when one child is speaking at any one time, may present fewer problems than the assessment of group discussion, but even this is not easy. The teacher has to consider such aspects as:

■ where he or she will sit during assessment. Should the teacher be in full view of the speaker, giving good eye contact and displaying appropriate 'listening' body language

while assessing, or should the teacher sit out of view so as not to inhibit the speaker? Answers to these questions will depend upon the nature of the talk and the individual preference of the speaker.

■ whether the teacher should take notes during the presentation or afterwards. Teachers who know their children well will be able to decide which is best for each individual child and of course the children might well be consulted about these considerations.

The practicalities of assessing children in group discussions deserves some attention. Perhaps the first issue that teachers need to consider is whether they can assess more than one child simultaneously. Doing so appears to be the answer to the perennial problem of lack of time. However, actually undertaking multiple assessments can be very tricky even for experienced teachers. It might be best to assess one child at a time at first until you are familiar with the assessment criteria and the layout of the recording sheet. As confidence grows, teachers may wish to attempt to assess two, or more, children at a time. Perhaps the answer is to simply note quotes from, and body language of, each child, which exemplify the focus of the assessment. These can be analysed later to assess the quality of each child's contribution. (See completed sample sheet on opposite page.)

▌Assessing listening

The interrelatedness of speaking and listening serves to further complicate the assessment process but assessing listening separately can often be a spurious and futile practice. Many teachers will want to gauge their children's listening by the spoken responses made during discussions or during/after formal speaking occasions. This seems highly preferable to asking children to write responses to prove that they have listened. This practice can often demean the listening process and can cause problems for children who can listen and respond very competently but who have trouble writing. However, assessing listening skills is necessary to provide children with accurate and focused advice for improvement. An assessment sheet with specific criteria for listening during group discussions and formal speaking activities is therefore provided on photocopiable page 26.

The main focus for assessment in this book is clearly on speaking and listening but given that the activities provided are always in a context, teachers may find that they are able to assess children's understanding of the science, history or geography concepts too. This is a bonus and will help to furnish teachers with further evidence of children's learning in other areas of the curriculum.

▌Assessing group discussion

The assessment of group discussion/talking and listening in groups often gives teachers cause for concern, mainly in relation to the ethereal nature of the discussion and the lack of hard evidence. Some of the issues raised by teachers are outlined in the following table. Strategies to help tackle the issues are also provided.

Issues	Potential solutions
Finding the time to assess every child	▌ Try to assess more than one child in the group. ▌ Focus on one particular aspect of group discussion. (This should help with the point above.) ▌ Incorporate assessment focus into forward plans. ▌ On occasions when timetabled to teach a group, use this time for assessment purposes. ▌ Focus on two or three children each week in a range of speaking and listening activities.
Lack of hard evidence	▌ Provide talk diaries* for each pupil. ▌ Assess outcomes which have been jointly devised, eg a group's final version of a 1960s pop song (see page 34). Take care, however, as this will not provide evidence of the process, which is the main focus here. ▌ Consider occasionally taping children, but only if practical and useful! ▌ Observe group with a clear focus for assessment. This should help to move beyond impressionistic assessment.
Involving children in the assessment	▌ Share purposes and expectations with the children. ▌ Provide feedback to the group following assessment. ▌ Interview the group after the activity. ▌ Develop self-assessment skills (see page 23). ▌ Develop group assessment skills (see page 24).
Managing other groups while assessing	▌ Allocate activities which children can undertake independently of the teacher. These might include reading, writing and practical tasks. ▌ Reinforce a 'no interruptions' rule while working on assessment.
The effects of teacher presence	▌ Be discreet and consider sitting near the group but not with the group. ▌ Incorporate assessment into activities on a more regular and formative basis. This should help children acclimatise to the process and your presence. ▌ (See also page 28.)

* Talk diaries can provide an overview of the range of opportunities for speaking and listening that a child has experienced. They should include a simple format for the child to keep a record of their involvement in speaking and listening activities. The diaries can help to raise the status of speaking and listening among pupils and parents. They can be a manageable and valuable resource when gathering evidence on a pupil's progress. A suggested layout is given on photocopiable page 27.

Photocopiable page 28 can be used to support your assessment of group discussion and listening in groups (see completed sample sheet right).

Assessing:

Group discussion ✔ Listening ☐ Drama ☐
Please tick

Date: _____ Topic: _____

Children in group	Examples of *justifying opinions*	Examples of *modifying point of view*	Summary
Anna	'I think it could be because the last time...' 'The reason I want to... is because...' 'If we do that then...'	'Yeah, that sounds like a great idea.' 'I think Fraser's idea about... sounds good.' 'So that means my way won't work?' Leaned towards speakers and gave good eye contact.	Dominated a little. Justified most opinions fairly well. Listened well to others and modified ideas with good grace.
Fraser	'Do you know why I think that? It's because...' 'Listen, I know it won't work because I tried it once when I was...'	'Oh yeah, I see what you mean! Nice one, Anna! So do we ditch Karen's suggestion? No, that won't work, silly!' Looked excitedly at others when he was speaking.	Justified with gusto! Listened well to others but should try to justify the rejection of others' ideas in a softer manner.
Karen	'I like that way best because it's best.'	'I agree with Anna.' Looked at all speakers and nodded a lot.	Offered few ideas and could not really justify any. Appeared to listen well but agreed with everyone.
Lorna		'No way. That's rubbish. No it isn't. That's not true.' Sighed a lot and looked away when others were speaking.	Offered no real opinions and disagreed with everyone. Appeared not to listen well or politely to others.

Future action for:
Anna. Model for Anna ways of encouraging others to speak.
Fraser. Offer some sentence starters to help Fraser deal politely with others' opinions.
Karen. Try similar activity but in a group of three chosen by Karen.
Lorna. Show Lorna the record of her quotes and explore whether she was less comfortable with the topic under discussion or the composition of the group.

▌Assessing drama

Some of the features of group discussion which make it difficult to assess also arise in the assessment of drama. For example, children are often involved in planning and performing as groups rather than individuals. In addition, the images children produce, by nature, lack permanence, making it difficult to obtain evidence of progression in learning. Clearly, therefore, some of the advice offered in undertaking assessment of group discussion may be useful in undertaking assessment in drama. This advice would be particularly relevant in relation to the following issues:

- finding the time to assess every child
- lack of hard evidence
- involving children in the assessment.

In addition to the strategies outlined previously, evidence of learning may be gathered from the sources outlined below. Obtaining evidence in this way enables what might otherwise be impressionistic assessment to be backed up by actual examples, such as how children are using space, sequencing material, using gestures, and so on. You may also find that photocopiable page 28 will support your assessment of objectives in drama.

Observation

Advice offered in group discussion in relation to finding the time to assess each child may be useful here (see page 21). Three or four children could be tracked against the objectives of the drama activity. Work of others, which is particularly significant, should be noted too.

Photographs

These are useful to capture still images and to record individual children's use of space, gestures, and so on.

Video and audio recording

These can be useful as a record of work in progress as well as a finished production.

Writing

This may take the form of a scripted scene or could be a piece of writing undertaken in role, for example a diary entry of one of the explorer's thoughts (see page 65).

Artwork

This could include a mask or prop which has been made for a drama activity. It could also take the form of a drawing of a character or setting in a drama.

Self-assessment

▌ The activity I have just completed was about:

Group discussion   **Listening**   **Drama**   **Speaking**

Please circle

▌ During the activity I was trying to practise the way I:

▌ I think I did this:

very well   **quite well**   **not as well as I would have liked**

Please circle

because:

▌ When practising this type of speaking/listening again I will try to:

▌ If I think I need help to do this I will:

■SCHOLASTIC

Group reflection

▌ What was it we were trying to do today?

▌ How well did we do this?

▌ Give an example of how we built on the opinions of others.

▌ When did we find it more difficult to reach an agreement?

▌ Give an example of someone in the group responding to others.

▌ What will we try to do to make the speaking and listening even better the next time we work together? Is there any help we need? (For example, when dealing with opposing views.)

Assessing speaking

Name: _____ Date: _____ Topic: _____

Aspect of speaking	Comments
Content ■ relevance of material to topic ■ relevance of material to listeners ■ appropriateness of vocabulary ■ appropriateness of syntax	
Delivery ■ audibility ■ clarity ■ pace ■ engagement of audience	
Logistics ■ use of visual aids ■ use of equipment ■ use of notes ■ positioning of self and visual aids	
Body language ■ stance ■ composure ■ scanning of audience ■ facial expression ■ gestures	

Next step for child:

SCHOLASTIC

Assessing listening

Name: _____ Date: _____ Topic: _____

Feature	Date: Activity:	Date: Activity:	Date: Activity:	Date: Activity:
Eye contact				
Body language				
Asks questions during/after activity				
Builds upon what has been heard				
Summarises main points				
Makes direct reference to what has been heard				
Uses what has been heard in order to predict				
Applies new knowledge to related activity				

Note: Not all the categories will be appropriate to all listening activities and sources (for example, radio, live presenter, audio cassette, video). It might be best to asterisk those categories that will be the focus for each assessment. For some features you may wish simply to tick to denote frequency. For others a brief comment about consistency or quality may be required. In other cases a direct quote or description of response may be helpful.

SCHOLASTIC

Talk diary

Keep a talk diary to record your involvement in speaking and listening activities:

▮ Decide whether the main focus for the activity is speaking, listening, group discussion or drama.

▮ Write down and complete the two starter sentences below which are linked to the focus of the activity.

▮ Add the date to your entry.

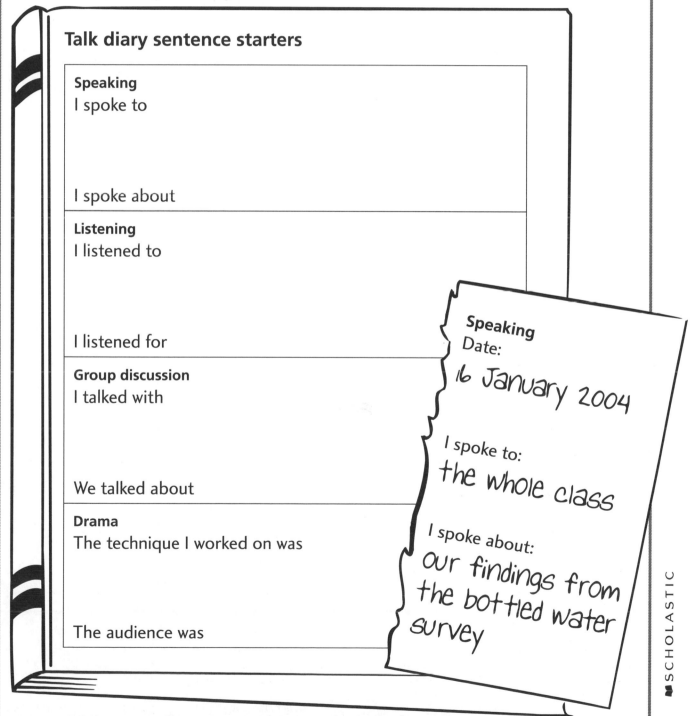

Talk diary sentence starters

Speaking

I spoke to

I spoke about

Listening

I listened to

I listened for

Group discussion

I talked with

We talked about

Drama

The technique I worked on was

The audience was

Speaking
Date:

16 January 2004

I spoke to:
the whole class

I spoke about:
our findings from the bottled water survey

SCHOLASTIC

Assessing:

Group discussion ☐   Listening ☐   Drama ☐
Please tick

Date: _____ Topic: _____

Children in group	Examples of *	Examples of *	Summary

Future action for:

* Teachers should add particular activity objectives here.

■ S C H O L A S T I C

The 1960s

Linked to
The National Curriculum for history, Key Stage 2, 'Britain since 1930';
Scottish environmental studies 5–14 guidelines, social subjects, 'People in the past'

Activity	speaking	listening	group discussion	drama
1. 1960s people photocopiable page 38	▌ show shape and organisation ▌ speak audibly and clearly	▌ ask relevant questions		▌ explore characters and issues
2. News of the decade photocopiable pages 39 and 40	▌ use vocabulary and syntax ▌ gain and maintain interest of audience ▌ choose relevant material ▌ show shape and organisation ▌ speak audibly and clearly ▌ evaluate speech		▌ make relevant contributions ▌ qualify or justify ▌ deal politely with opposing views ▌ help the group to move forward	▌ explore characters and issues
3. 1960s pop songs photocopiable page 41		▌ identify gist/ key points ▌ respond to others	▌ make relevant contributions ▌ vary contributions ▌ qualify or justify ▌ deal politely with opposing views ▌ help the group to move forward	
4. A street game		▌ ask relevant questions ▌ respond to others	▌ make relevant contributions ▌ vary contributions ▌ deal politely with opposing views ▌ help the group to move forward	▌ create, adapt, sustain different roles ▌ use character, action, narrative to convey ideas
5. Groovy! photocopiable pages 42 and 43	▌ speak audibly and clearly ▌ evaluate speech	▌ identify gist/ key points ▌ recall important features	▌ make relevant contributions ▌ qualify or justify ▌ deal politely with opposing views	▌ create, adapt, sustain different roles ▌ evaluate contributions

1960s people

Objectives

❚ To ask and answer relevant questions in order to gather facts

❚ To prepare a talk using information gathered through research

You will need

❚ Photocopiable page 38

❚ Information texts related to the 1960s

Activity time

1 hour

Assessment

❚ Were relevant questions asked?

❚ How successful was the child in sustaining a role?

❚ How well organised was the talk? Was the child able to make use of their original notes to help them to shape their talk?

Background information

This activity supports children as they research 1960s characters, then clarifies and refines their understanding through hot-seating and a prepared talk. In order for the focus to be clearly on speaking and listening, work related to the reading and writing aspects of this activity should be undertaken as part of children's personal research, as a homework task or during a previous lesson.

What to do

Organise the children into groups and give each child a copy of photocopiable page 38. Tell the children to allocate 1960s personalities featured on the page to individuals in their groups (this is likely to motivate children more effectively than being told which personality to research). Ask the children to research their personality and to fill in the appropriate spaces on the central grid. Encourage them to use a wide range of non-fiction texts and the Internet to gather their information. Other personalities may be substituted for those included on photocopiable page 38.

Ask the children to return to their groups. Each child in the group should now have information on a different 1960s personality. Provide each child with further copies of the photocopiable sheet, stapled together, to complete. First ask the children to use the information they have gathered from researching their particular personality to take it in turns to be in the 'hot seat', answering questions in role from the rest of their group. The earlier research work will make the exercise of hot-seating more productive, giving the children sufficient resources to draw on when speaking. If children have not had much experience of this technique, go into the hot seat yourself to demonstrate how to get into role, and how to answer questions appropriately. (For further advice on the technique of hot-seating, see page 15.) Spend time modelling how to frame questions using the headings suggested on the sheet, for example when interviewing 'Mary Quant' and for *Profession*

a question could be *What kind of job do you do, Mary?* or *What line of work are you in, Mary?* Ask the children to fill in one sheet for each personality being interviewed. Once these steps have been explained to the children, withdraw to let them undertake the activity, intervening only if turn-taking procedures need reinforcement.

If children are showing real interest in the personalities then you may wish to ask each child to prepare a two-minute talk about their 1960s personality, using notes made during their original research as support. The headings on photocopiable page 38 will provide a useful structure for children's talk, and their hot-seating experience will have helped them to clarify their thoughts.

Consider possible audiences for this talk beforehand so that the material children choose to present is relevant to the listeners. Ask the children to select one relevant picture related to their 1960s personality from books, magazines, newspapers or the Internet to support their talk. If resources permit, have this put onto an overhead transparency. Suggest that children make a note of when the picture may be used most effectively in their talk. Plan in time for the children to rehearse their talk.

Simplifying the activity
■ Allocate 1960s personalities to the children.
■ Remove the requirement to take notes on photocopiable page 38 during the hot-seating activity.
■ Put the children into groups of three, during hot-seating and presentation activities, to make the listening and speaking less onerous.

Extending the activity
■ Encourage the children to ask questions beyond ones relating to the categories given on photocopiable page 38.
■ Suggest that children prepare and present their talk on one of the other personalities researched in their group.
■ Invite some children to present their talk using only notes, if you feel this is appropriate.

News of the decade

Objectives
▌ To choose and shape texts for a short presentation

▌ To speak audibly and clearly and in standard English during the presentation

▌ To sustain roles during the presentation

You will need
▌ Photocopiable pages 39 and 40

▌ Reference books with photographs related to the events

Activity time
3 hours

Assessment
▌ Look out for children using appropriate actions and voice intonations in keeping with the roles of announcer/reporter.

▌ Have 'announcers' used standard English with clarity and brevity?

Background information
This activity involves a group of children in examining a variety of texts about events that took place in the 1960s and choosing four out of six to present to an audience. Children are invited to consider certain aspects of each text and are guided in their discussion by the use of a comments sheet.

This activity might best be undertaken near to the end of the topic when children will have some background information about each subject. This would increase their confidence and engagement with the task. It is anticipated that this lesson may be undertaken over a few days.

Other children may be involved in the presentation, for example choosing appropriate music for the introduction, background music for each item, the finale of the presentation. Others could be asked to decide upon the clothes, hairstyles and make up of the presenters.

What to do
Explain to the group that the whole class will be making a 'News of the decade' presentation and that they have to choose four out of the six items (Beatlemania, Flower power, The Vietnam War, Fashion, Civil rights, China's cultural revolution) to present to an audience. Inform the children that the presentation will take the form of a television news programme complete with announcers and reports from different people or interviews.

Provide each member of the group with copies of photocopiable pages 39 and 40, and offer reference books on the 1960s. Explain

to the children that they should read the first text on photocopiable page 39 before discussing it in their group, then move on to the next text and do the same. Photocopiable page 40 has been designed to guide their discussions at each stage of their decision-making and to help them to come to a considered agreement.

After the children have completed the table on photocopiable page 40, they should decide on the four items that they want to include in the presentation. The texts they choose should be adapted in light of the comments they have made on photocopiable page 40 about the length of the text and the language used. (You might decide to split the group into pairs to work on each text to adapt it.)

The children should now consider the order of presentation of the items, and may need your guidance on this. For example, if they have chosen the Vietnam War, Civil rights, Fashion and Beatlemania will the first two serious items appear consecutively or should they be separated from each other by one of the other less serious items? Should they start on a serious note? Should they end on a serious note? What do they think their audience would want?

Once the order has been decided, two 'anchor people' should be chosen to devise short appropriate introductions and linking sentences between the items. Give the children examples here of appropriate/ inappropriate links (for example, ask them: *Which sounds best: 'And now over to our correspondent in San Franciso' or 'Let's hear from John who is our correspondent in San Francisco and who has been watching some hippies at a pop festival over there'?*).

It is important to offer children a very tight time limit for each presentation, for example no more than ten seconds for each introduction and three minutes per report.

There will be some children who should now plan the logistics of their part of the presentation, including finding appropriate photos from reference books to back up their texts and making cue cards, if these are being used. Children should decide who will undertake the speaking and who will change the photos or operate the cue cards. They might decide whether they will be 'in the studio', presenting, or reporting from 'on the scene'.

The Vietnam War

Children will need time to rehearse their presentation and should be encouraged to note on their script places to pause, when to refer to photos, and so on. They should also consider and practise appropriate intonations and facial expressions in keeping with the nature of the item. Encourage the children to watch news programmes at home and to note the use of standard English, tone of voice and facial expressions of the announcers and reporters. They should also be encouraged to seek help with pronunciation of any unfamiliar or difficult words.

Newsreaders from the group should now come together to present their 'News of the decade' broadcast to the rest of the class.

Simplifying the activity

■ Fewer texts might be examined by the group, with the teacher or other adult scribing the adaptations.

Extending the activity

■ Children could be asked to decide on one or two other 1960s news items to be included. They could then write their own scripts, using texts and photos from reference books, the Internet or other sources.

1960s pop songs

Objectives
▌ To make suggestions and listen to alternatives

▌ To achieve compromise when necessary

You will need
▌ Photocopiable page 41

▌ A recording of the song 'Waterloo Sunset' by Ray Davies recorded by The Kinks (optional)

Activity time
45 minutes

Assessment
▌ Were alternatives considered in an effort to reach agreement?

▌ What strategies did children use to reach a compromise?

Background information
Here, the children are given the lyrics of a 1960s song presented in the wrong order and are challenged to put them in the right order. This is a useful way of 'Talking about texts' (Scottish English language 5–14 guidelines), and having some fun! It is likely that the song that is the focus for the activity will be unfamiliar to the children but this might depend on the age of children's parents or grandparents.

What to do
Before groups work on their own to sequence the song on photocopiable page 41, demonstrate, using a different song from the one the children will use, the kind of clues that they can look for to aid their sequencing. For example, you could try to establish whether there is a narrative running through the lyrics, or whether there are syntactic clues which would help.

Issue an enlarged copy of photocopiable page 41, cut into different sections, to each group. Give the children time to consider different ways in which the song might be sequenced. Model how to listen to each other's ideas and reach a compromise, for example *I think Laura's right because the song might finish with a line that has the title in it; I still think the first line is _____ , but I see what you mean about _____; Let's go with Lisa's idea about _____ .* Each part of the song has been given a letter and it might be helpful for children to keep a record of the alternatives they have tried to let them return to a previous, possibly more effective sequence. This strategy might also encourage them to consider other options by giving them the security of knowing they can return to an earlier version.

Once the children have considered and discussed alternatives, provide each group with the real version for them to check their sequence. Seeing a copy of the song and hearing how it sounds is a useful and novel way for children to check their 'answers'. (The correct order is C, F, B, E, H, A, D, G.)

Simplifying the activity
▨ Consider providing the children with some lines from the song which have already been sequenced for them.

Extending the activity
▨ Try the activity again but with a 1960s pop song which has a less obvious structure, for example 'Dedicated Follower of Fashion', another song by The Kinks.
▨ Ask groups to select a song of their choosing and try the activity out with others (including teachers and parents!).

A street game

Background information

Hopscotch, originally played by children in Ancient Greece and Rome, was a popular street and playground game in the 1960s. Today it is still played all over the world.

Rules can vary from country to country. Usually, the first player tosses a small stone or other object (for example, a beanbag), into square one of a grid. If it does not land in the designated square, the player forfeits his or her turn. If successful, the player hops on one foot over the lines from square to square (starting at square one) to the end of the grid, then hops back through the squares, stopping to pick up the stone while standing on one foot in the nearest square to the one in which the stone has landed. He or she then hops out of the grid. The player then repeats the process, throwing their stone into square two. If, while hopping through the grid in either direction, a player steps on a line, misses a square, puts two feet down or falls over, their turn finishes. That player must start with the same square on his or her next turn. The first player to complete one successful set of hops for every numbered square wins.

In this activity, groups work together to devise rules for a new version of the game.

What to do

If you have a grid for this game painted on the school playground, take the children outside to demonstrate how it is played (see above). If not, use chalk to mark out a large hopscotch grid on the ground (see grid 1). Or clear a space in the classroom and use masking tape on the floor.

Put the children into groups of four. Ask them to share ideas about possible ways to adapt the game, using a 3 x 3 grid (see grid 2). Provide a practice and demonstration area for groups. (If further space is available, several other grids similar to grid 2 should be marked out.) Encourage the children to give each group member time to explain their ideas. Demonstrate ways in which they can make constructive comments and build on others' ideas, for example *What about taking Anna's idea about using a _____ but make it for four people rather than two? Or I think that sounds a great idea, but it might be a bit complicated. Can anyone think of a way to make Sajid's plan a little easier?*

Emphasise that it may not be one person's idea that the group decides to develop but a combination of different parts of individual ideas. Allow time for this exploratory talk before asking children to write out the rules for their game.

Exchange each group's rules with those from another group and direct the children to play the game according to the rules provided. Encourage children to make notes about the set of rules related to:
- things they like
- things they do not understand
- things which might improve the game.

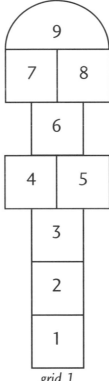

grid 1

Objectives
❚ To make relevant suggestions and respond to those of others

❚ To convey feelings sensitively in relation to different issues arising during a game

You will need
❚ Paper for planning

❚ Chalk or masking tape (if required) for grid

❚ An object, such as a flat metal tin or plastic box, for moving round the grid

Activity time
1 hour

Assessment
❚ To what extent were children able to listen attentively to the ideas of others?

❚ Were children able to make positive comments in relation to other groups' games?

❚ What strategies did children use to offer critical comments in constructive ways?

❚ How successful were children in resolving incidents arising during games?

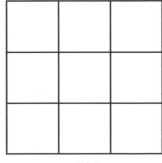

grid 2

When they have done this, bring the groups back together and ask each group to take it in turns to provide feedback. The notes the group has made related to the three aspects previously outlined should provide the basis for the feedback from one group to the other.

Once feedback has been discussed, direct the children to their original groups to revise the rules in relation to the feedback they have received. If possible, make use of the gym area for groups to play their new 'hopscotch' game.

Simplifying the activity
■ Appoint a chairperson to ensure everyone's ideas are heard.

Extending the activity
■ Ask children to suggest 'incidents' which might occur when the game is being played, for example someone removes the stone, someone does not follow the rules, someone goes into a huff over a comment made by another player. Put these suggestions onto 'incident' cards and issue one to a child in each group. Ask these children to follow what the card tells them to do (see sample card right) without letting the others in their group know. Direct the group to play the game and to negotiate to resolve the incident when it arises.

Incident card 1
The 'hopscotch' game is underway but you have been left out. You always play with the children in this group and don't know why they have asked someone else to take your place. You approach the group and your opening line is: 'Can I play in the next game?'

Groovy!

Background information
This activity involves children in 'translating' 1960s words and phrases into ones that would be more appropriate today. They are required to carry out a little homework before undertaking the activity by asking those who grew up in the 1960s about the meanings of some of the words and phrases. It is meant to be fairly light-hearted, and parents and carers may enjoy being involved in the preparatory stage. Not every child in the group activity need translate all the words and phrases. The purpose here is to share findings and to work out meanings together.

What to do
Issue a copy of photocopiable page 42 to the children, asking them to take it home to find out the meaning of the 1960s words and phrases. If this is not possible, they can simply ask adults in the school. Tell the children that they need not find translations for all the words and phrases, and that they can add to the list if they come across other 1960s words or phrases.

In their groups, let the children take turns to share responses and add to their lists. Then they should tick the 1960s words or phrases that are still in use today. Do they mean the same today as they did then?

Now give the children copies of photocopiable page 43, explaining that the first paragraph of text is typical of the type of words and phrases used in the 1960s. Ask the children to 'translate' it into standard English. Point out that each group's translation might be very different from other groups and that this is fine; what is important is that the children should have grasped the gist of the story. Allow one child to read the 1960s paragraph, phrase by phrase, while another child translates each phrase into standard English.

The children are now ready to translate the paragraph that uses standard English into 1960s style language. Again stress that translations will differ.

Simplifying the activity
■ Ask the children to match the 1960s words to the standard English words on photocopiable page 43 using photocopiable page 42.
■ Provide the children with the first photocopiable page only (page 42) and encourage them to use 1960s phrases during the week in class, whenever they feel it would be fun!

Extending the activity
■ Allow the children to dress up for the translation performance, with one child in 1960s fashion and the other in more sober clothes!
■ Children could incorporate words and phrases from the 1960s into reports they write of any interesting findings about this period.

Objectives
▌ To explore changing vocabulary and syntax

▌ To identify the gist of some text

▌ To create and sustain a role

You will need
▌ Adults who are old enough to have lived through the 1960s!

▌ Photocopiable pages 42 and 43

▌ Information texts related to the 1960s

Activity time
30 minutes per activity

Assessment
▌ Were children able to understand the meaning of the paragraph using 1960s words and phrases?

▌ Could they adopt and sustain different roles when using standard English and 1960s words and phrases?

1960s people

John F Kennedy

Dr Martin Luther King

Valentina Tereshkova

Paul McCartney

Mary Quant

Neil Armstrong

Name of personality	Date of birth
Profession	Place of birth

Main achievement	

Alive?	If alive, where now?

Other information	

News of the decade (1)

1. Beatlemania

The four mop heads from Liverpool, namely John Lennon, Paul McCartney, George Harrison and Ringo Starr, took the world by storm. Their particular brand of music was new and exciting, and the youth of the world adored it. During Beatles' concerts the audience would scream, cry and swoon as the band tried to perform.

Their songs were translated into various languages and they topped the 'hit parade' of most countries as soon as they were released.

Pop merchandising reached its peak with the Beatles. There were Beatles' mugs, lamps, wallpaper, wigs, suits, jewellery, pencils, chewing gum. It seemed that any object could be turned into a Beatles' object.

2. Flower power

"Peace and love, man" was the greeting of the hippies. These peace-loving people were normally young folk who were disaffected with the way that politicians and others were running the world. They believed in having few rules in society and wanted everyone to live in harmony. Many hippies wore loose clothes with floral or psychedelic patterns. Both male and female hippies wore their hair long and often adorned it with flowers.

Hippies protested about the Vietnam War and indeed any war. Many young people of the 1960s dressed like hippies but not all took part in anti-war rallies or believed in world peace.

3. The Vietnam War

By 1969, about 550,000 Americans were involved in the war between North and South Vietnam. America supported South Vietnam against the communist North. Massive bombing raids were launched against the North but despite America's superior weaponry the North could not be defeated. The North used guerrilla tactics. The average age of an American soldier in Vietnam was 19. Peace talks began in 1968 and led to America's withdrawal in 1973. The terrible sufferings of the war caused many Americans to lose faith in their government and many people protested against the war. The youth of the world appeared to be united in the belief that this war was unnecessary.

4. Fashion

The teenagers of the 1960s looked to music and fashion to express their identities and to emphasise the difference between them and their parents. Sixties' fashion moved from formality and uniformity to colour and fun. Many men wore ties that matched the pattern of their shirts. Skirts were shorter (miniskirts) or long and flowing.

The most influential British designer was Mary Quant, who not only invented the miniskirt but also introduced tights as a fashion necessity. She often used black and white geometric shapes in her designs.

Floral patterns were also very popular in clothes but not the realistic patterns that the older generation was used to. The flowers were highly stylised and 'psychedelic'.

5. Civil rights

In America in the 1960s, civil rights activists worked to win equality for black people, particularly in the southern states. Many states operated a policy of segregation. This involved keeping black and white people separated in schools, housing and many public places including buses. The most influential campaigner for civil rights was Dr Martin Luther King, a black Baptist minister. Dr King was often arrested and beaten but despite this he maintained a policy of non-violence. He was awarded the Nobel Peace Prize in 1964. Dr King was murdered in 1968 and his unjust death caused widespread rioting among black people in US cities.

6. China's cultural revolution

During the 1960s, China underwent revolution. Under the leadership of Mao Tse-tung China broke away from its communist neighbour, the Soviet Union.

Mao believed that the state should be owned by the workers and the peasants. He trained young men and women, known as Red Guards, and ensured that government officials, university staff and other 'privileged workers' were put to work in the fields and factories. By 1968, however, disruption was so great that the army stepped in to restore order and the cultural revolution ended.

SCHOLASTIC

News of the decade (2)

▌ Rate the interest to audience: High →Average →Low. Why do you think this?

▌ Language: are there difficult words? Are some words too 'babyish' for the audience? Are some sentences too long?

▌ Is the text too long? Too short? What could you do about this?

▌ Put a tick next to the four texts you want to include in the presentation. Decide on an order for the texts.

Text	Comments	Position in talk
Beatlemania		
Flower power		
The Vietnam War		
Fashion		
Civil rights		
China's cultural revolution		

▌ On the back of this sheet, explain why you have decided on the order you have chosen, for example We have put x first because… The next item is x because…

Waterloo Sunset

A

Every day I look at the world from my window
Chilly chilliest evening time, Waterloo sunset's fine.

B

Every day I look at the world from my window,
Chilly chilliest evening time, Waterloo sunset's fine.

C

Dirty old river, must you keep rolling, rolling into the night,
People so busy, make me feel dizzy, taxi lights shine so bright,

D

Millions of people swarming like flies round Waterloo underground,
Terry and Julie cross over the river where they feel safe and sound

E

Terry meets Julie, Waterloo Station, every Friday night,
But I am so lazy, don't want to wander, I stay at home at night,

F

But I don't need no friends
As long as I gaze on Waterloo Sunset, I am in paradise.

G

And they don't need no friends
As long as they gaze on Waterloo Sunset, they are in paradise

H

But I don't feel afraid
As long as I gaze on Waterloo Sunset, I am in paradise.

Groovy

■ Match the 1960s words to the present day words. Some of the 60s words mean almost the same thing, so you may have to write some more than once.

1960s	2000s
a happening	
fab	
gear	
good/bad scene	
groovin'	
guy	
let it all hang out!	
split	
uncool	
with it	
hip	

1960s	2000s
chick	
dig it	
get on down	
cool	
swinging	
cool cat	
boutique	
hangin' out	
hey man	
groovy	
square	
chill out	

Today's words

girl/young woman, boy/young man, enjoy/like it, enjoy yourself, fashionable, exciting, fashionable person, clothes shop, relaxing with, unfashionable, hello there, party/event, wonderful, clothes/accessories, good/ bad event, relaxing, relax!, leave, join in, great, pleasant, relaxed person, understand it, dancing

What does it mean?

▌Can you translate this into standard English?

I was hangin' out in a café when this really cool cat came in who was wearing really fab gear. He made the rest of us look square. "Hey man!" he said, "There's a happening tonight at Dave's. Do you dig it?"

When we got to the happening, some cats were already groovin' to the music, others were just chilling out. All us chicks and cats had a really swingin' time but I had to split before the others, which was uncool.

▌Can you translate this into 1960s language?

The end of term party was really exciting. The hall looked amazing. Everyone wore their best clothes and even the teachers looked fashionable for once! The music was wonderful and everyone joined in the dancing. It was a really great event.

Linked to
The National Curriculum for history, Key Stage 2, 'European study of Ancient Greece'; Scottish environmental studies 5–14 guidelines, social subjects, 'People in the past'

Ancient Greece

Activity	speaking	listening	group discussion	drama
1. Creating your own Greek god photocopiable pages 52 and 53		▌ ask relevant questions ▌ respond to others	▌ make relevant contributions ▌ qualify or justify ▌ deal politely with opposing views ▌ help the group to move forward	
2. Mottoes for the gods photocopiable page 54		▌ ask relevant questions ▌ respond to others	▌ make relevant contributions ▌ qualify or justify ▌ deal politely with opposing views	
3. It's a myth photocopiable page 55	▌ speak audibly and clearly ▌ gain and maintain interest of audience	▌ ask relevant questions ▌ respond to others	▌ make relevant contributions ▌ qualify or justify ▌ deal politely with opposing views	
4. Dramatising the myth photocopiable page 56		▌ ask relevant questions ▌ respond to others	▌ make relevant contributions ▌ qualify or justify ▌ deal politely with opposing views ▌ help the group to move forward	▌ create, adapt, sustain different roles ▌ explore characters and issues ▌ evaluate contributions
5. Olympic debate photocopiable pages 57 and 58	▌ speak audibly and clearly ▌ show shape and organisation	▌ ask relevant questions ▌ respond to others ▌ identify gist/key points ▌ recall important features ▌ identify language features for specific purposes	▌ ask relevant questions ▌ respond to others ▌ identify gist/key points ▌ recall important features ▌ identify language features for specific purposes	▌ make relevant contributions ▌ qualify or justify ▌ deal politely with opposing views ▌ help the group to move forward

Creating your own Greek god

Objectives
▌ To reach decisions

▌ To make an oral presentation using an appropriate style of language

Background information
It might be best to undertake this activity with children after they have acquired a little background knowledge of some of the Greek gods. In this activity pairs of children are asked to create their own modern gods according to given criteria. They then create a short oral presentation in keeping with the persona of the god they have created.

You will need
▌ Photocopiable pages 52 and 53

▌ Card and paints for making masks

▌ Pictures and information on Greek gods

What to do

Show the children pictures of some Greek gods and recap on their names and deeds. Ask them whether they think the images of the gods match their deeds. Point out that not all gods were good or wholesome.

Discuss the children's favourite Greek gods and why they appeal. Discuss what gods had in common (most were powerful; patrons of something; and have one main deed for which they are known).

Ask the children what kind of god they would create today if they had the power. Can they think in terms of everyday life and problems that the modern gods would address? Children might offer various suggestions at this point. Provide them with further ideas by distributing cards made using copies of photocopiable page 52. Allow the children to choose from the cards or issue particular cards to pairs of children. You could offer each pair a choice of, for example, four cards. Some children may prefer to use their own ideas or focus on a smaller detail, for example if they have *clothes* on their card they could choose to be the god of trousers rather than the god of *all* clothes.

When they know who their god will be, issue each pair of children with a copy of photocopiable page 53, which should help them to consider their god in much more detail. Explain that space has been left for notes on details relating to their god before they make their final decisions. Some children

Activity time
1 hour 50 minutes

Assessment
▌ Did children justify their decisions to one another?

▌ Did they reach decisions in a polite way?

▌ Did they use appropriate voices and language during the presentation?

Zeus, Museum of Olympia, Greece

might benefit from drawing their god after considering points one to eight. Indeed this might be the point when children stop to make a mask of their god for use in the oral presentation. This will help them to identify with their god and to consider the subsequent points in more depth.

Note: the decisions about the name and the family tree of the gods have been left until the end. This should help children to reflect on the chosen features of the god before choosing a name that reflects those features. The family tree might help to make an interesting extension to this activity (see below).

After children have made their final decisions you might want to ask them to use their completed table to plan a draft of their oral presentation. Provide sentence starters such as *I am called... I have the ability to... When I am angry* for children who need help with this.

Children can then wear their masks for the final presentation. It might be that one child of each pair wears the mask while the other gives the oral presentation. This child should decide whether to use notes or to learn their lines by heart.

Simplifying the activity

■ Children can discuss fewer features on photocopiable page 53 and then make masks for display only.

■ Read aloud the choices given for the draft of the oral presentation and allow children to choose from options, then scribe their final draft with them.

Extending the activity

■ Ask pairs of children to get together with other pairs to make up a family of gods. Who should be the mother/the father/the brothers/sisters? Who was first born? Each family should present, one after the other. This might give the oral presentations some coherence for the audience. Children will have to plan and agree the wording of the links.

Mottoes for the gods

Background information
This task follows on from the previous activity in which children created their own modern day Greek god. Here, children are asked to make a motto for their god. (It might be best to ask children to collect mottoes during the week or so before they undertake the activity. Parents/carers' help might also be enlisted.)

The features of a good motto are addressed, and children are asked to discuss the merits of given mottoes before devising one for their god.

What to do
Ask the children to look at their completed table related to the features of their Greek god (see photocopiable page 53). Recap on a few of these and tell the children that they are now going to add another piece of information. They will be devising a motto which can be associated with their god.

Tell the children that the motto for the modern Olympic games is *Swifter, Higher, Stronger.* Display a few of the mottoes that the children have collected and discuss with them what they have in common. Emphasise that most have few words; some can give succinct advice (for example, *Be Prepared*); they are sometimes inspirational (for example, *Onwards and Upwards*) and are often related to ideas behind an organisation (for example, *Per Ardua Ad Astra* – the RAF's motto meaning 'Through Adversity to the Stars').

Issue a copy of photocopiable page 54 to each pair of children and ask them to rate each motto before planning and devising their own. Next, ask each pair to join with another two pairs, and ask each in turn to present their mask from the previous activity and to recap on their god's features before revealing their motto. The other two pairs should discuss their motto and offer one piece of advice for improvement. The pair can decide whether to accept or reject the advice.

Display the final mottoes beside the children's masks of their gods.

Simplifying the activity
■ Omit the peer criticisms and advice.

Extending the activity
■ Ask the children to devise three mottoes and to undertake a survey of their friends/relations to decide on the final version. Children could construct a recording sheet for this survey.

Objectives
▌ To justify their decisions

▌ To listen to others' advice and make amendments in the light of criticisms

You will need
▌ Photocopiable page 54

Activity time
45 minutes

Assessment
▌ Did children justify their decisions to others?

▌ Did children give and take advice/criticism with good grace?

It's a myth

Objectives
▌ To take turns to exchange information through speaking, listening and note-taking

▌ To negotiate and reach agreement in an appropriate manner

You will need
▌ Photocopiable page 55

▌ A range of myths

Activity time
1 hour

Assessment
▌ Were children able to take turns appropriately to exchange information?

▌ How successfully did children negotiate and reach agreement in the ideas associated with the myth?

Background information
In this activity, which builds on 'Creating your own Greek god' (see page 45), the children are asked to write a myth based on rivalry between two gods originally created by themselves. These myths will be presented in the next activity, 'Dramatising the myth' (see page 49).

What to do
Read examples of myths to the children. From these recap on the features of myths. For example, myths:
- are fiction
- often address a problem concerning human existence
- usually contain supernatural elements
- can be similar to fables and fairy tales
- can be linked to popular ideas about natural phenomena
- sometimes contain a moral.

Ask the children to return to the pairs they were in for the activity, 'Creating your own Greek god'. Explain that they are now going to think about a myth that they could build around the details that they have already created.

In groups of four, the children should now exchange information about the gods they have created and plan their myth, basing it on a contest between the two gods. Issue them with a copy of photocopiable page 55 on which they can plan their ideas. Offer them some linguistic structures to help them compromise to create a joint myth, for example *I like your idea for the reason for the argument and I think we should use that; I think my suggestion about where the contest took place is better because…; Why don't we choose a different judge for the contest because we don't agree about…?*

After the myths have been written, ask pairs of children to read their myths to each other and to reflect on and compare the interpretations of each of the myths. To support them in doing this in a constructive manner, suggest that they make use of phrases such as *I like what you decided the gods argued about, it fits in well with the types of gods; Your ending was really good. It came as a surprise.*

Simplifying the activity
■ Shorten the planning frame and number of questions on photocopiable page 55.

Extending the activity
■ Encourage the children to write their own myths which incorporate their ideas about characters, setting and plot, without the need for a planning frame.

■ Provide copies of myths for groups and ask them to suggest three common features based on their reading.

Dramatising the myth

Background information
It is important that groups have created their myth before undertaking this activity (see previous activity) in which they dramatise it.

What to do
Organise the children into the groups of four they were in for the 'It's a myth' activity (see page 48). Ask them to identify three key moments from each pair's myth. Emphasise that these moments should relate to the argument, the contest and the outcome (see photocopiable page 55). If necessary, help the children by taking one of their myths as an example and outlining three possible key moments.

Discuss with the children how meaning can be expressed through taking up different positions and employing a range of facial expressions. For example, hands on hips, legs wide apart and furrowed eyebrows may denote anger. The group should now illustrate each of their key moments in their myth through freeze frames (see page 15). Encourage them to plan the positions and facial expressions they will adopt for each key moment to create three still pictures of the two gods. The children should note down their ideas on a sheet of paper.

Encourage the pairs in each group to take it in turns to offer constructive comments about the portrayal of the gods at each moment, suggesting ideas for improvement. Model the feedback by suggesting sentence starters, such as *I liked the expression on your face during the contest; You followed the ideas about the position you were to take during the argument; What about putting your head in your hands at the end as well as…?* Ask the children to make a note of any changes they wish to make.

Give the children guidance about how long

Objectives
▌ To consider how meaning and impact can be expressed through posture and facial expression

▌ To collaborate to identify dramatic ways of conveying character and ideas

▌ To modify ideas in light of feedback

You will need
▌ Photocopiable page 56

▌ Children's comics showing thought bubbles for characters

Activity time
1 hour 45 minutes

Assessment
▌ Were children able to express meaning and create impact through posture and facial expression (and later with the addition of a character's thoughts)?

▌ How successfully did children collaborate to identify dramatic ways of conveying character and ideas?

▌ To what extent did children modify ideas in light of feedback received?

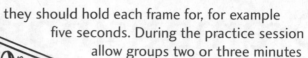

they should hold each frame for, for example five seconds. During the practice session allow groups two or three minutes after each frame to discuss the synchronisation of the positions. Direct groups to practise putting the three frames together. Show the children how to 'melt' one freeze frame into another in a slow and controlled manner. Encourage the children to modify their plans based on this discussion.

Give each group an opportunity to present their freeze frames to the others in the class. Encourage the audience to speculate about characters and ideas being expressed through the positions and facial expressions of each of the frames.

In their groups, the children should work out the thoughts of both gods during each of the freeze frames. Remind the children that the frames will only be held for five to seven seconds so the 'thoughts', when they are spoken, need to fit into this length of time. They should record their ideas on photocopiable page 56. Do not be surprised if some children begin to write dialogue rather than thoughts. Use some examples from children's comics to exemplify 'thoughts' here. Ask the children to decide who will take up the positions of the gods in the freeze frames and who will say the thoughts. Give children time to practise adding the thoughts to the frames.

Ask the children to discuss whose thoughts will be spoken first, and how they will be spoken, for each of the frames. Children should note their decisions in the *Directions* column of the thoughts plan on the photocopiable sheet. Provide time for children to practise adding thoughts to the frames and to make modifications to their plans.

Give each group an opportunity to present their extended freeze frames to the others in the class.

Simplifying the activity
■ Omit the addition of thoughts to the freeze frames.

Extending the activity
■ Encourage groups to select their own key moments for the freeze frames.
■ Extend the number of key moments for the freeze frames.
■ Provide a wider audience for the freeze-frame presentations.

Olympic debate

Background information
This activity involves children planning and carrying out a debate about the value of
competitive games. One group of four plans the 'for' presentation and one group of four
plans the 'against' presentation. All other children are the audience. You may wish to inform
those children who will be presenting the arguments of the subject of the debate in advance
to give them time to reflect, read and talk about it with parents and others. It might be best
to allow children who have had little experience of debates to decide for themselves whether
to talk 'for' or 'against' the subject.

What to do
Decide which group of children will be speaking 'for' and which group
will be speaking 'against' the motion: *This class believes that competition
is a good thing.* Split each group of four into pairs and ask them to
come up with at least three reasons for their stance on the motion.
Now ask each pair to join up again to collate their responses. This
snowballing (see page 14) might increase the responses.

Now issue each group of four with one half of photocopiable page
57, the half containing the points for the opposing motion. This should
help them to prepare counter arguments.

Each group is now ready to plan their argument. Issue photocopiable
page 58, which will help the children to structure their presentation
and to use language that might persuade the audience to vote for
them. The children will need time to prepare their presentation and
it might be best to set aside time to listen to children's rehearsals
in order to offer constructive criticism about the structure and the
language. The children should decide who will present each argument.

Before the debate takes place, explain to the children that the
presenters will be using language to persuade them to think as they do.
Can they spot the phrases that they are using? Ask them to note down
these phrases while they are listening. Encourage the children to think
of points that they would like to add or questions that they could ask
after the presentations, and to note these down also.

If children are unfamiliar with debating you may want to chair the
debate yourself, otherwise a child can be appointed.

Now set up the debate with the 'for' group presenting first. At the
end, questions should be taken before moving to a vote.

Simplifying the activity
■ Offer children three or four reasons for or against the motion and
ask them to structure their presentation around these points.

Extending the activity
■ Ask presenters to make concluding remarks before moving to a vote.
■ Ask them to incorporate one (or two) points that were raised during
the debate in their concluding remarks.

Objectives
▌ To persuade others of a point
of view

▌ To listen for and note
persuasive language techniques

You will need
▌ Photocopiable pages 57 and 58

▌ Paper for note-taking

Activity time
1 hour 30 minutes

Assessment
▌ Could children incorporate/
adapt the persuasive language
techniques to good effect?

▌ Did children structure their
presentations appropriately?

▌ Did they listen for and note the
persuasive language being used?

The god of…

clothes	music	electrical appliances
food	games	fashion accessories
TV programmes	weather	drink
feelings	time of day	teachers
moods	colours	animals
singing	dancing	hair
bathrooms	kitchens	sweets
the Internet	computers	dreams
CDs	text messages	mobile phones

Creating your own Greek god

Features
1. What are you the god of?
2. Are you the god of all _____ or are you the god of a particular aspect of _____?
3. Male/female?
4. Your hair
5. Your face
6. Your height
7. Your clothes
8. Any special powers?
9. What angers you?
10 What do you do when angered?
11. What pleases you?
12. How do you reward those mortals who please you?
13. What is your name?
14. Who is your mother/father?
15. Do you have any brothers/sisters? Their names?

■SCHOLASTIC

Mottoes for the gods

■ Give each of these mottoes a mark out of 10.

Healthy Eating
Eat well, live well ☐

We should always eat a lot of fruit and vegetables if we want to be healthy and strong ☐

Olympic Games
Swifter, Higher, Stronger ☐

Compete to be the very best athlete in the Games ☐

A school
Love learning ☐

You should work hard and enjoy all lessons if you can ☐

Car Breakdown Service
If your car breaks down we will get to you very quickly ☐

We get there first ☐

Boy Scouts
Boy scouts are friendly and are often ready to help everyone ☐

Be prepared ☐

■ Now tick the kind of motto you want for your god.

We want our god's motto to give advice to others. ☐

We want our god's motto to inspire others. ☐

We want our god's motto to boast about her/his powers. ☐

Remember:
- **Mottoes use as few words as possible.**
- **Mottoes often use words that are memorable.**
- **Mottoes can give very short pieces of advice.**
- **Mottoes can inspire others.**
- **Mottoes can tell people something about you.**

■ Now write your motto in no more than six words.

_____

It's a myth

▌ You know your own god well, but use the notes about the other god to help you make decisions about the things included in the planner below. Use the planner as the outline for your myth.

Name of my god	**Name of other god**
Key features of god	Key features of other god

What did they argue about?
Where did the contest take place?
Who judged the contest?
Who watched the contest?
What happened during the contest?
What happened as a result of the contest?

Dramatising the myth

▌ Use this grid to plan the thoughts of your gods, and how they will be spoken.

Freeze frame 1

The contest

	Thoughts	Directions
god A		
god B		

Freeze frame 2

The argument

	Thoughts	Directions
god A		
god B		

Freeze frame 3

The outcome

	Thoughts	Directions
god A		
god B		

Photocopiable

Your group is *against* competitive games.

The other group may offer you the following reasons why they are *for* competitive games:
■ They help people to try really hard to beat others.
■ They make people strive to improve their own performance.
■ They are very exciting to watch.
■ Spectators love to support particular competitors.
■ It feels great when your team/competitor wins.
■ They are very exciting to take part in.
■ Winners feel great knowing that they are the best at their game.

Your own ideas:

Olympic debate

Your group is *for* competitive games.

The other group may offer you the following reasons why they are *against* competitive games:
■ They make people selfish because they care only about themselves winning.
■ They do not help the nations of the world to work together and live in peace.
■ Some people may start to dislike the people of a country which beats their country.
■ Some athletes want to win so much that they are tempted to take drugs to enhance their performance.
■ More people lose than win in competitive games.
■ Losers may feel ashamed, depressed or angry.
■ Winning can encourage people to boast and gloat.

Your own ideas:

Preparing your speech

■ Your group want to convince the audience to vote for your opinion. Try to use language that will persuade the audience. The following phrases may help you to convince others!

Hints for structuring your speech:
■ State your opinion briefly at the beginning.
■ State one point that you agree with at a time and try to give an example of each.
■ Take two or three points that others might say and say why you disagree with each one.
■ Use short sentences as often as possible.
■ Sum up, using short sentences.

Phrases that might be useful

Think about it very carefully...

You know it makes sense...

Of course everyone feels that...

Some may say... but let's think about that a little more.

It is very important to consider...

Competition is crazy (if against). Competition is cool (if in favour).

Just think of a time when...

We feel very strongly that...

We want you to vote for us not because you like us but because...

Exploration and discovery

Linked to
The National Curriculum for history, Key Stage 2, 'Britain and the wider world in Tudor times'; Scottish environmental studies 5–14 guidelines, social subjects, 'People in the past'

Activity	speaking	listening	group discussion	drama
1. To boldly go… photocopiable page 66		▌ask relevant questions ▌respond to others	▌make relevant contributions ▌qualify or justify ▌deal politely with opposing views	
2. Hopes and fears photocopiable pages 67–9		▌ask relevant questions ▌respond to others	▌make relevant contributions ▌qualify or justify ▌deal politely with opposing views	
3. Fair trade photocopiable page 70		▌ask relevant questions ▌respond to others	▌make relevant contributions ▌vary contributions ▌deal politely with opposing views ▌help the group to move forward	▌explore characters and issues
4. An explorer's thoughts photocopiable pages 71 and 72	▌speak audibly and clearly	▌ask relevant questions ▌respond to others	▌make relevant contributions ▌qualify or justify ▌deal politely with opposing views	▌explore characters and issues

To boldly go…

Objectives
❚ To challenge, support and respond to others' contributions

❚ To prioritise options after weighing up a range of opinions

❚ To achieve a compromise when necessary

You will need
❚ Photocopiable page 66

❚ Blank cards

❚ Large sheets of paper

Activity time
45 minutes

Assessment
❚ To what extent were children able to challenge, support and respond to others' contributions?

❚ Were groups able to prioritise options after weighing up a range of opinions?

❚ Were children able to compromise?

Background information
This activity is not related to any particular time period, but encourages children to examine in a global way why individuals and groups take risks to explore areas unknown to them.

What to do
Issue each group with a copy of photocopiable page 66 (cut up into sections to facilitate discussion). Explain that this offers some suggestions about why people explore. Ask each group to read the suggestions and encourage them to use blank cards to add their own suggestions.

Ask the children to discuss each of the suggestions, including their own, and reach a consensus about what they think are the six most likely reasons for people exploring. Take this a step further by directing groups to arrange their six reasons in pyramid fashion, with their most likely reason at the top, and the others in descending order.

Model language which will help children to agree or disagree with others' ideas, for example *I agree with what Fraser said about…; I partly agree with Mai Lee's reason for putting _____ in our top three; I'm not sure about… but…* This will help them to seek clarification about others' ideas, for example *Did you mean…? Could you say that again, I'm not sure what you mean by…*

Give each group a large sheet of paper on which to record their main reason for people undertaking exploration. They should complete the following sentence: *People explore mainly…*

Organise groups for 'envoying' techniques here (see page 14). Ask each 'envoy' to find out if any other reason for exploring has been added by the group. If so, ask them to note what it is and return to their group with it for discussion, with a view to adding it to their list or discarding it. Bring the class together and ask each group for their concluding sentence. Encourage each group to look for similarities and differences among the reasons, and to ask each other questions regarding the choices they have made.

e. To gain information about the world

d. To meet new people/ influence others

h. To find out about animals and plants

a. To have a better standard of living

g. To have an adventure

i. To achieve a goal

Simplifying the activity
■ Stop the activity after the six reasons have been chosen by the group, before any prioritising is done.

■ Give only four options to prioritise.

Extending the activity
■ Ask each group to display their priority pyramids. This will allow comparison of ideas beyond only the main reason for exploration.

Hopes and fears

Background information
In this activity, children are given the opportunity to examine the hopes and fears of inexperienced sailors during Tudor times, an age of discovery and exploration. (You may wish to choose another period.) It is designed to help them to examine their assumptions about travelling to an unknown island and to help them empathise with explorers of the past. The point is made that the journey itself held more danger than the land to which they travelled.

What to do
Organise the children into groups of approximately four. You may want to split the class into two, each undertaking one of the tasks, then comparing their findings with each other. Tell the children to imagine that they are a group of young people who have never sailed before – they have never left their own town and know little of the world. (You could give children names in keeping with the particular time period.) Explain that, as this group of people, they are all going to travel on board the sailing ship *Trust* bound for an island called Cupra. Point out that this group of people know very little about geography, so being told exactly where they are going to be travelling to will make no real sense to them; they have only heard that Cupra is hot. (You may want to customise the name of the ship and island to suit the period/place you are studying.)

Provide the children with an enlarged copy of photocopiable page 67 and ask them to talk about each aspect of the island in turn. What will they hope to find? What might they be afraid of? Explain that it is not necessary to have a fear for every feature they discuss, and that they can be as optimistic or as pessimistic as they wish. Ask one person from the group to note-take on the photocopiable sheet. Children should conclude their discussion by ticking one of the boxes at the bottom of the sheet and completing the starter sentences, *The thing that we hope for most is…* and *The thing that we fear most is…* When they have

Objectives
▌ To make relevant contributions during group discussion

▌ To listen and respond to others' opinions

▌ To use freeze frames to explore feelings

You will need
▌ Photocopiable pages 67–9

▌ Reference books about life on board sailing ships during Tudor times (or your chosen period)

▌ Word cards and hat/container

Activity time
1 hour 30 minutes plus research time

Assessment
▌ Did children listen to everyone's views before drawing conclusions?

▌ Were opinions justified by referring to prior knowledge?

▌ Were freeze frames portrayed with attention to details of posture and expression?

finished talking, present them with the 'answers' on photocopiable page 68. Discuss the answers and ask the children to tell you if they were surprised by any of them.

Now distribute enlarged copies of photocopiable page 69, which enables children to address the conditions on board the ship *Trust*, together with reference books about sailing ships during Tudor times or the period you are studying. Explain to the children that they should discuss each feature of life on board ship and take notes, as before. They should then take time to research the features before completing the third column of the photocopiable sheet. (You may want children to break into pairs to research a few of the features.)

When the children have done their research, ask them to come together to share their findings before comparing these to their initial speculations noted on photocopiable page 69.

Explain that they are now going to freeze-frame the first meeting between explorers and islanders. For the freeze-frame activity (see page 15), you may want to split the class into three groups of eight, then split each group of eight into two groups of four, with four children being explorers and four being islanders.

Put some word cards into a hat. Each card should have a different emotion or feeling written on it, such as *hostile, friendly, a little afraid, arrogant, apprehensive* (make sure that you duplicate some of them, as both islanders and explorers may share the same feelings!). Allow each group to choose a card from the hat and to practise stance, posture and facial expressions that best match the emotion on their card. Now bring together the groups of explorers and islanders, so that they are in their original groups of eight. Ask one of the groups to display their freeze frames simultaneously, as if they have just met each other for the first time. Other groups should watch this and try to decide on the feeling each group is portraying. After all three groups have displayed their freeze frames, the class can discuss which they think would be the most likely scenario in real life.

Simplifying the activity
■ Adapt photocopiable pages 67 and 69 so that the children discuss fewer aspects.
■ Do *either* the features of Cupra or life on board *Trust*.
■ Give 'answers' to the children for the last column of photocopiable page 69, rather than expecting them to do their own research about what life would have been like on board *Trust*.

Extending the activity
■ Let the *children* decide on the features of Cupra and/or life on board *Trust* that will be discussed in their group.
■ Ask the children to make a presentation of their findings to other groups or another class.
■ Challenge the children to make a true/false quiz about life on board ships for other groups to answer.

Fair trade

Background information
This activity provides children with the opportunity to discuss an ethical issue, of which they have some awareness, in a different and more sensitive context. They will need to understand that:
▌ for an exchange or trade to be fair it needs to be something that the other person wants or needs
▌ some things are regarded as too valuable to be exchanged or traded.

What to do
Before the children undertake the activity, talk with them about what criteria they use when exchanging or swapping toys, games, books or cards. Raise the question of what constitutes a fair or an unfair swap in these situations. Establish the points mentioned above.

Organise the children into groups and provide each group with a copy of the scenario (copied and cut out from the first part of photocopiable page 70) and the cards (copied and cut out from the bottom of photocopiable page 70). Ask the children to read the scenario, then to read the options on each card. Explain that the cards offer some options for trading with the islanders, but that groups should be encouraged to add other options themselves (provide blank cards for this). Give the children time to discuss each of the options in their group.

Once the children have discussed each option, explain how the fair/unfair continuum works. (Taken from the middle of photocopiable page 70, it would be helpful to have this enlarged for each group.) Then leave them to discuss where each card should be placed on the continuum (where they place a card on the line that runs from *not fair* to *very fair* will depend on how fair their group think the trade is).

Objectives
▌ To challenge, support and move on others' contributions

▌ To make decisions effectively

▌ To explore the idea of a moral dilemma through a dramatic technique

You will need
▌ Photocopiable page 70

▌ Blank cards

Activity time
1 hour 30 minutes

Assessment
▌ Were children able to challenge, support and move on others' contributions in a useful and polite manner?

▌ Did children make decisions after considering as many options as possible?

▌ Were children able to make suggestions to increase the effectiveness of the conscience alley technique?

Emphasise that groups should be able to offer reasons for the decisions they have made. As with the 'To boldly go…' activity (see page 60), revisit language which will help children to agree or disagree with others' ideas, for example *I agree with…; partly agree with…; I'm not sure about… but*, and so on. Other than responding with some points of clarification regarding the scenario, try not to intervene in their discussion.

When the children have made final decisions about where their cards should be placed, ask them to complete the sentences related to the fairest trade and the trade they have decided to make. In some cases these might not be one and the same thing!

Display the groups' ideas about what they think is the fairest trade and what trade they have decided to make. Encourage the children to question any decisions which they think are unfair.

Explore with the class some of the thoughts which crew members might have had as they began to trade with the islanders. Read the scenario again with the children, then brainstorm thoughts from a 'fair-minded' viewpoint first, for example *Help the islanders and they will help you; the plants are precious to the island*. Then brainstorm some thoughts from an 'unfair' viewpoint, for example *Just give them the beads, they like them; we could come back later when no one is here and just take the plants*. Record the children's ideas for use later on.

Use the children's ideas to undertake the drama technique of conscience alley (further details can be found on page 16). Nominate one child to be the captain from the ship. Put the class into two lines, one line taking a fair viewpoint and the other line taking an unfair viewpoint. As the captain walks between the two lines, each child should call out some of the thoughts the captain of the ship may be experiencing. Work with the children to make decisions about:
- the pitch of the 'thoughts'
- how the thoughts should alternate from line to line
- whether some of the thoughts should be spoken by more than one child
- whether some of the thoughts should be repeated.

After reflection on these aspects, change the 'captain' and repeat the process.

Simplifying the activity
- Provide less detail and fewer points in the scenario on photocopiable page 70; cut down on the number of options from which the children can choose when making decisions about which trade is the fairest and which trade they have decided to make.

Extending the activity
- Increase the number of options.
- Suggest that groups write out six options of their own.

An explorer's thoughts

Background information
This activity helps children to discuss similarities and differences between the thoughts and feelings of an explorer during Tudor times and the Age of Discovery, and an astronaut today. Children are supported in deciding on whether the feelings of explorers presented to them are more pertinent to the past or to the present. They are also guided to consider which feelings would be common to both 'then' and 'now'.

What to do
Before working on this activity, allow the children to carry out research of their own on the feelings of early explorers and of present day astronauts.

Cut out the thought bubbles on photocopiable page 71 and put them in an envelope (you will need a set for each group). Divide an A3 sheet of paper into three columns, with the headings *Then*, *Both* and *Now*. Prepare one sheet for each group. Give an envelope of thought bubbles and a prepared A3 sheet to each group. In groups of four, children should discuss each thought in turn to decide whether it is apt for the *Then*, *Both* or *Now* column.

After the children have put their thought bubbles into the different categories, encourage them to write more thoughts of their own on blank bubbles and to add these to the appropriate column.

Explain to the children that they are now going to plan a presentation called 'An explorer's thoughts (past and present)', with one child acting as a sailor of the past and another as an astronaut today. The use of simple costumes or symbolic props (for example, stars on a backdrop for the astronaut and waves on a backdrop for the sailor) could be discussed and made by the children to enhance the presentation. Distribute enlarged copies of photocopiable page 72, which will help the children to plan the structure and content of their presentation, considering all the issues. They may need to be reminded of communal voice and thought-tracking techniques (see page 16) before they begin.

Simplifying the activity
■ Ask the children simply to place the thought bubbles under the *Then*, *Both* and *Now* headings, without adding their own.
■ Omit the presentation.

Extending the activity
■ Suggest that the children write their own ideas for the explorer's thoughts before categorising them into *Then*, *Both* and *Now*.

Objectives
▌ To justify decisions to other members of the group

▌ To plan an oral presentation with others and to speak clearly and audibly during the presentation

▌ To make a presentation, using communal voice and thought-tracking techniques

You will need
▌ Photocopiable pages 71 and 72

▌ Blank thought bubbles and envelopes

▌ Frieze paper and paint

▌ Information books about life on board sailing ships of the past and spaceships today

Activity time
1 hour 35 minutes

Assessment
▌ Did children justify their decisions to other members of the group?

▌ Did children deal well with opposing opinions/viewpoints?

▌ Did children act upon advice given about how voices sounded during rehearsals?

To boldly go

Why do people explore?

a. To have a better standard of living

b. To trade

c. To live/settle

d. To meet new people/ influence others

e. To gain information about the world

f. To test a theory

g. To have an adventure

h. To find out about animals and plants

i. To achieve a goal

j. To do something different

Hopes and fears about Cupra

▌ You are a group of young people who want to sail to Cupra on the sailing ship *Trust*. Talk about what you think the island might be like.
Discuss each feature in turn. One person should take notes.

Feature	What we hope to find	What we fear about this
Climate		
Physical features – forests, deserts…		
Vegetation		
Animals		
Size of the island		
People (hostile or friendly?)		
How the people survive		
Celebrations		

We have more hopes than fears about the island of Cupra. ☐
We have more fears than hopes about the island of Cupra. ☐
Complete the sentences on the back of this sheet:
The thing that we hope for most is… The thing that we fear most is…

SCHOLASTIC

The island of Cupra

Climate
Hot summers and fairly mild winters. The rainy season is at the beginning of summer. North of the island is cooler than the south.

Vegetation
Very green and fertile land in the north. Special plants grow here. Dry barren south.

Animals
Snakes (not poisonous) and small lizards. Parrots. Cats and dogs as pets.

Size of the island
10 000 square km (approximately).

How the people survive
By cultivating the fertile land of the north which grows bananas, coconuts and almonds. By gathering the water that melts from the mountain tops and flows down the mountain sides.

Physical features
One major active volcano in the north of the island. Fertile land around the volcano. Mountain range in the north. Ice from the mountain tops produces the only water source.

People (hostile or friendly?)
Neither hostile nor friendly. They are excellent farmers and want to trade with us but they are a little suspicious of us. Many other travellers have tried to cheat them before.

Celebrations
Birthdays are celebrated by giving gifts and eating special cakes. The volcano is celebrated at the first full moon after the first rains. The celebration involves music, food and dancing outdoors from midnight until sunrise.

Hopes and fears about the journey on ship

Feature	What we hope to find	What we fear about this	What we have found out
			(This column is to be completed later.)
Food			
Water			
Beds			
Medical help			
Toilet facilities			
Work for new sailors			
Relaxation/ pastimes			
Any other feature			

We have more hopes than fears about sailing aboard *Trust*. ☐

We have more fears than hopes about sailing aboard *Trust*. ☐

■ Complete the sentences on the back of this sheet:
The thing that we hope for most is…
The thing that we fear most is…

■ SCHOLASTIC

Fair trade

The island of Cupra is the only known source of a plant called Scaratona, which is known to cure serious skin conditions. One of the reasons we have travelled to the island is to trade with the islanders for the plant. Although the plant grows fairly successfully on the island, its growth can be put at risk by extremes in the weather, which the island can experience from time to time. As a result of this, the islanders carefully harvest the seeds from the plants, and young plants are grown to replace those that are dying.

You are prepared to trade some gold for some of the seeds that have been harvested. However, the islanders have shown great interest in a bag of glass beads that one of the crewmen has brought from part of the cargo on board ship. In light of this interest some of the people who have accompanied you to the island are encouraging you to trade the glass beads instead of the gold.

In the meantime, you have noticed that many of the homes are in a poor state of repair. The islanders are aware of this problem and know how to fix their homes but they are busy working on other important projects.

The trade we think is fairest is _____.

The trade we have decided to make is _____.

Not fair						Very fair
1.	2.	3.	4.	5.	6.	7.

a. We give gold and take the seeds and the young plants.	b. We give glass beads and take the seeds, but leave the young plants.	c. We give gold and glass beads and take the seeds and the young plants.	d. We offer to fix the homes, and take the seeds and the young plants.

An explorer's thoughts

I won't be able to talk to my family.

I'll be one of the first humans to see this place.

I'll be travelling for many months, perhaps years.

People back home will worry about me.

Going to the toilet may be tricky.

Conditions on board will be cramped.

I'll feel very proud of myself when we reach the destination.

I won't have fresh food to eat.

I may not have a lot to eat on board.

There will be lots of work to keep me busy.

I'll enjoy the company of others when I'm on board.

SCHOLASTIC

Planning the presentation

Questions	Our decisions	Things we will need to do
In your group decide who should be the sailor and who should be the astronaut. Don't just vote, justify why these people would be appropriate for the parts.		
Decide whether you want the actors to speak their thoughts aloud or whether other people should do this behind the scenes. Why have you decided this?		
How will you order the thoughts? Will all the thoughts be used? Will all the astronaut's thoughts be heard first, then the sailors? Or will they take turns? Why?		
Should there be a presenter/ narrator? If so, what will he or she say?		
Do you want to undertake the 'communal voice' technique here? How many will speak for each explorer?		
What props might you need to help your audience enjoy the presentation?		
How long might you need to rehearse the presentation? When might you do this?		
Do you want anyone's advice about how the voices sound before you present? Whose advice?		

SCHOLASTIC

Traffic in the high street

Linked to
The National Curriculum for geography, Key Stage 2, 'Managing environments sustainably';
Scottish environmental studies 5–14 guidelines, social subjects, 'People and place';
The National Literacy Strategy *Framework for Teaching*, 'Persuasive writing'

Activity	speaking	listening	group discussion	drama
1. Leave the car – take the bus photocopiable page 82		▌respond to others	▌make relevant contributions ▌qualify or justify ▌deal politely with opposing views ▌help the group to move forward	
2. Betty's buses photocopiable page 83		▌ask relevant questions ▌respond to others	▌make relevant contributions ▌vary contributions ▌qualify or justify ▌deal politely with opposing views ▌help the group to move forward	
3. Noisy routes		▌respond to others ▌recall important features	▌qualify or justify	
4. Location, location, location	▌show shape and organisation	▌respond to others	▌qualify or justify	
5. Pedestrian precinct problem photocopiable pages 84 and 85	▌speak audibly and clearly ▌gain and maintain interest of audience ▌show shape and organisation	▌respond to others	▌make relevant contributions ▌qualify or justify ▌deal politely with opposing views	▌create, adapt, sustain different roles

Leave the car – take the bus

Objectives
▌ To offer and accept ideas unconditionally during a brainstorming session

▌ To allocate tasks and undertake procedures as agreed in the group

You will need
▌ Photocopiable page 82

Activity time
1 hour 30 minutes

Assessment
▌ To what extent were children willing to offer and accept ideas during the brainstorming session?

▌ How successfully were they able to agree and follow procedures agreed for the collation of survey results?

Background information
In this activity children are asked to consider incentives which might encourage more people to use buses and trains, thereby reducing congestion and pollution. As a starting point, the activity focuses on special offers on goods and services, of which children are likely to have had some experience.

What to do
Introduce the concept of businesses making use of incentives to encourage the public to buy or make use of their products and services more often. Demonstrate how to undertake the technique of brainstorming (see page 14) by asking the children to tell you about special offers and gimmicks that they have come across themselves, for example in the context of cinema tickets or take-away food. Prompt them to consider offers and gimmicks such as *cheaper before 7pm*; *free toy with meal* and so on.

Now ask the children, in their groups, to brainstorm special offers

and gimmicks which might encourage people to use buses and trains more often. Before they start, remind them to accept everyone's ideas at this stage. Then ask the children to compare their ideas with those listed on photocopiable page 82, ticking off those they have included in their brainstorm.

Now bring the class together and collate any ideas groups have included in their brainstorm which do not appear on the list on the photocopiable sheet. Work with the class to select the six incentives from the amended list that they think might encourage more people to use public transport. This will help to sift out some of the weaker ideas that groups may have come up with, for example free travel. It is important to agree on a common list of incentives in order for comparisons to be able to be made from the survey results.

Explain to the children that they will now seek the views of others through a survey to establish which offers will encourage different groups of people to use public transport. Ask the groups to write down the common list of six incentives on the survey sheet on photocopiable page 82. Split the class into three broad sets to survey:

■ people at school
■ people at work
■ people who are retired.

When the surveys have been returned, ask the groups to plan an efficient way of collating the results. Suggest that children might, for example, work in pairs within the group to aid the collation, with one child reading out responses and the other keeping a tally on an unused survey sheet. Model ways of negotiating responsibilities within the group, for example *Who wants to…? I wouldn't mind doing… I think we should do _____ before _____. What do you think?*

Ask each group to review their findings, reach a conclusion and read their concluding sentence (on photocopiable page 82) to others. Collate the findings from all the groups and highlight similarities and differences among the three sets of people surveyed. Ask the children if they are surprised by any of the results.

Point out to the children that if their survey results are to have an effect then they need to inform local bus, train and underground companies about their recommendations. Try to obtain a different local company for each group to contact by letter or e-mail. Model how their communication with the company could be structured, for example:

■ introduction explaining who the children are and the purpose of the investigation
■ the most popular incentives for groups 1, 2 and 3
■ a concluding paragraph including inviting the company to offer a response.

Simplifying the activity

■ Suggest that the children select four ideas from the given list and add them to the survey sheet.
■ Ask the children to undertake the survey on a general basis rather than with specific sets of people.

Extending the activity

■ Do not put forward different sets of people for groups to survey. Encourage the children to add a space for age and direct them to organise their responses into three broad age groups themselves.

Betty's buses

Objectives
▌ To reach a consensus after considering individual preferences

▌ To use agreed features to make judgements

You will need
Photocopiable page 83

Activity time
45 minutes

Assessment
▌ How successfully did children reach a consensus after considering individual preferences?

▌ To what extent did children make use of agreed features to make judgements?

<table>
<tr><td>

Background information
This activity provides children with opportunities to talk about texts and examine particular features of language which can be associated with advertising. Selecting the features that children like in a slogan will help the group to enjoy a more objective discussion and achieve some consensus.
</td></tr>
</table>

What to do
Initiate a class discussion about what makes an effective slogan by outlining and discussing some well-known slogans, for example *Just do it; Va va Voom; You know when you've been Tangoed; You have more fun with Maltesers; It's good to talk.* Encourage the children to say which ones they like and why. Ask them to compare their ideas with the possible features suggested below. A slogan might include:
■ no more than six words
■ the name of the company
■ some alliteration
■ some rhyme
■ some rhythm
■ some humour.

Organise the children into groups and issue copies of photocopiable page 83. Ask each group to decide on the three features that they think are important in a good slogan. (It would help groups to make their choices if some well-known slogans and a sample list of features were clearly displayed for the children to refer to.) Direct them to the top of the photocopiable sheet where they should note down the three features they have decided upon.

Explain to the children that a local bus company is seeking advice about some slogans their employees have devised to encourage greater use of their particular bus company. The children should read the slogans offered on photocopiable page 83 and make decisions on the effectiveness of each slogan by judging it against the features already decided upon by the group. Encourage the children to take turns to say the slogans aloud, and direct the others in each group to listen and identify the language features used. Suggest that they make notes on the photocopiable sheet in the comments section after hearing each slogan to help them to keep track of their discussion about each one. They should give each slogan a mark out of ten.

Model how to use the features they have decided on to judge each of the slogans, for example *I think this slogan is the best so far because it has all of the things we thought a good slogan should have; do we agree that this slogan should only get one point because it only has one of the features we chose? What mark should we give this one? We all like it but it has more than six words…* Do not be surprised if groups drift towards slogans which do not in fact display any of their chosen features. If this is the case, ask them to modify their chosen features or justify what it is they like about that particular slogan. Direct each group to reach a decision about the slogan they would advise the company to use and to complete the concluding sentence on the photocopiable sheet.

Bring the class together and compare similarities and differences among the choices made either by displaying the concluding sentences from each group or displaying the top three slogans from each group. Does there seem to be a preference for particular language features, for example alliteration? Or are preferences more widely spread among and within groups?

Simplifying the activity
■ Provide three simple features for the group to use as a basis for judging the slogans on photocopiable page 83 (see suggestions on opposite page).
■ Reduce the number of slogans that the children need to assess.

Extending the activity
■ Allow the children to add their own slogans created by the group.
■ Ask the children to modify some of the given slogans to improve them.
■ Encourage the children to review their original decisions about what makes a good slogan, having looked at the effectiveness of slogans that make use of other features.

Noisy routes

Objectives
▮ To justify their reasons for their decisions

▮ To negotiate

▮ To listen for and to identify specific sounds

You will need
▮ A sequence of photos of the shops/services in the local high street

▮ A cassette recorder with microphone and tape

Activity time
2 hours

Assessment
▮ Did children justify, with conviction, their reasons for including certain sounds?

▮ Was the route negotiated politely?

▮ Did those children who played the game listen attentively and identify specific sounds?

Background information
This activity involves children devising a game in which they plan a route along the local high street. They choose a sequence of aural signposts in the high street by recording appropriate sounds at given points. Other children have to listen carefully to determine the route taken.

What to do
Before this activity is undertaken, take a sequence of photos of both sides of the local main street. (A classroom assistant may be able to do this for you, or you could ask the children for help with taking photographs provided they are supervised.) The photos should then be joined together to make two separate long photos of the street.

Tell the children about the game they are going to create a couple of weeks in advance of the activity. This will give them time to listen out for particular sounds when they next visit their high street.

Set the scene by asking the children if they think they could guess where they were in the high street if they had their eyes shut. What might give them clues? What *particular* sounds would come from which points? Are there other points in the high street that would have particular sounds, for example the place where the newspaper vendor stands? The pedestrian crossing? The bus stop? You may find that children's mental map of the high street is a little hazy even if they visit it regularly.

Show the children the long photographs of each side of the high street, explaining that smaller photos have been joined together to show two continuous pictures. Tell them that they are going to make

a listening game for others to play. After planning a route, they will go out into the high street and record very particular sounds that emanate from precise points in the street. Children should choose a given number of sounds to record – enough to make the game interesting but not too many to be confusing. Other children can then look at the photos while listening to the sounds and decide which route has been taken.

The children should now go out (with adult supervision) and record the sounds in the order that they decided. You may want the whole class to undertake this in groups at the same time. It might be less problematic to allow children to make their route in groups of four or so throughout the week before others are asked to play it.

On their return to the classroom, the children should try out the game for any hitches that might require the route to be amended before giving the photos and recording to others to play.

Simplifying the activity

■ A classroom assistant could record the sounds that the children have decided upon (but this is not as much fun for children as doing it for themselves!).

■ Limit the sounds to three on either side of the street.

Extending the activity

■ Instead of using photos, provide the children with squared paper to make a simple diagram of each side of the street. Each shop or service can be indicated by a given number of squares (for example, four squares for small shops, eight squares for larger shops). Each shop should be named or coded. Other children can then be given the street diagram and the tape to listen to and should mark various points on the diagram (1, 2, 3 and so on) to denote the route taken.

Location, location, location

Objectives
❚ To use appropriate language to justify choices

❚ To listen to and respond to others' suggestions when negotiating

You will need
❚ Large maps of the local area

Activity time
15 minutes per group discussion and 3 minutes per group presentation

Assessment
❚ How frequently did children use appropriate language to justify their choices?

❚ How successful were their negotiating skills?

Background information
This activity should encourage children to discuss the pros and cons of particular locations for a new pedestrian crossing in the high street. Provided they are given a map of the surrounding area, they should be able to use their knowledge of the local area to make informed decisions.

What to do
Organise the children into groups of approximately four. Ask them to imagine that they are town planners who have to decide on the best location for a pedestrian crossing in the town. Issue each group with a large map of the local area, with locations A–G marked on it (each map should be identical).

Tell the children to list pros and cons for each site and that each child should take notes. Recap on note-taking at this point, emphasising the need to write only key words and to use abbreviations, where possible. Tell the children that once they have completed their own list they should reach a majority decision with their group on the site for the new pedestrian crossing. You might wish to encourage children to justify their decisions. Model phrases such as *The reason I think site A is better than site B is…* or *My two main reasons for voting for this site are…* or *Can I explain why I think that won't work?*

Two groups should now come together to compare findings and to reach a joint decision. At this point you may wish to sit with one group to model listening and responding to others' suggestions by using appropriate negotiating language, for example *Yes, I'll go with your decision here even though I think it should be the other one* or *If I accept Jack's point, will the group accept my decision on site D?* or *Yes that makes sense, I've changed my mind.* Each group should collaborate on a sentence or two that explains where they think the crossing should go and why.

Now ask a spokesperson from each group to present their group's reasons for choosing the site. Note the groups' decisions on the board and come to a final class decision.

Simplifying the activity
■ Ask each group to consider only three sites rather than seven.
■ Provide the children with cards on which you have written phrases that are useful when negotiating, such as *I hadn't thought of that* or *Perhaps you were right on that point*, and invite the children to choose a few to have to hand in their discussions.

Pedestrian precinct problem

Background information
This activity involves children in researching and discussing a traffic problem, then using persuasive language to argue their point of view.

What to do
Give the children the following imaginary scenario: the local high street is to become a pedestrian precinct (or if this is already the case, say that it may shortly be opened again to traffic). Explain that they are going to decide on what they believe is best for most citizens of their town. Divide the children into 'expert' groups (see page 14) of pedestrians, car owners, small shopkeepers, and managers of large stores that have their own car parks. Issue copies of photocopiable page 84 to help them with ideas. Explain that they should note down which statements they agree with (for example, *Shopping will be more relaxed*) and which ones they disagree with. Encourage them to come up with statements of their own. They should then agree upon the two main points they want to emphasise and the position they will adopt to present to the others.

Now issue copies of photocopiable page 85 to help them shape the short presentation they will give to others. You may want to sit with a group to model use of persuasive language, talking through the examples on the photocopiable sheet (*Shopping will be like walking through a sunny glade*, and so on) and encouraging the children to offer other examples. Decide whether they will be able to listen to all the presentations on one day or whether you would rather stagger the presentations throughout the week.

During each presentation, ask the children to listen carefully to identify the particular language devices that are being used. They could refer to the features listed on photocopiable page 85. Encourage each group to state the most appealing aspect of the presentations and to give one piece of advice to the presenters.

Simplifying the activity
■ Give the children specific examples (related to their role) of each language feature to choose from when they are using photocopiable page 85.

Extending the activity
■ Children could devise their own feedback sheet.

Objectives
▌ To shape an oral presentation

▌ To identify and use features of persuasive language

▌ To gain and maintain the interest of an audience while sustaining a role

You will need
▌ Photocopiable pages 84 and 85

Activity time
1 hour plus time to rehearse the presentation; 2 minutes per presentation

Assessment
▌ Did the children make good use of persuasive language techniques in their talk?

▌ Could they identify persuasive techniques used by others?

▌ How did they try to keep the interest of their audience?

Leave the car – take the bus

▌ This table shows incentives for people to use public transport. Did you think of any of these ideas in your group brainstorm? Tick which ones.

3 for the price of 2	
more routes	
buy one, get one free	
weekly ticket (cheaper than single journeys)	
more frequent service	
points for each journey (exchangeable for…)	
cleaner, more comfortable buses/trains	
children under 12 go free	

Survey

Write down your agreed list of incentives. Ask people to tick which one they think is the most important.

	Incentives	
1		
2		
3		
4		
5		
6		

Our group found that the main thing which would encourage more people who are at school, at work, retired* to use public transport more often was

* delete groups not appropriate

Betty's buses

We think a good slogan should include:

■ _____

■ _____

■ _____

Slogan	Comments	Mark
1. Betty's buses, better by far		
2. East, west, Betty's best		
3. Quicker, cleaner, no one cheaper		
4. For work or fun, Betty's the one		
5. Save time, save money, take Betty's		
6. Relieve the stress. Go Betty's, pay less		
7. Board Betty's buses		
8. Betty's buses – simply the best		
9. Betty's brilliant buses		
10. Good news – Betty's are in business		

We would advise the bus company to use _____

_____

as a slogan because _____

_____

SCHOLASTIC

Issues to consider

The traffic is dangerous.

The cars and buses pollute the air of the high street.

The bus stops are too far from the shops.

The traffic moves very slowly through the high street.

A pedestrian precinct is safer for children.

People who use wheelchairs can shop more easily.

It is very noisy in the high street with buses and cars passing through it.

Some older people cannot walk from the bus stops to the shops.

Shopping will be more relaxed.

The traffic brings customers to the shops.

Children will forget about using the Green Cross Code.

People will have to walk to the bus stops with heavy shopping.

BAKERY
BANK
CHEMIST
CLOTHES
MUSIC
SHOES

How shall I say it?

▌ Choose two or three of these ways of using language to persuade others to agree with you.

Feature	Example	How we will use this in our presentation
simple present tense	It is important...	
imagery	Shopping will be like walking through a sunny glade/through a nightmare of...	
alliteration	Exquisite experience, crushing crowds...	
address the listener	You know you want to... Can you remember when...?	
imperative	Just do it! Sit up and listen! Think about it!	

■SCHOLASTIC

Linked to
The National Curriculum for geography, Key Stage 2, 'Water and its effects on landscapes and people, including the physical features of coasts';
Scottish environmental studies 5–14 guidelines, social subjects, 'People and place'

Coastal holidays

Activity	speaking	listening	group discussion	drama
1. What is a coast? photocopiable page 94		▌ask relevant questions ▌respond to others	▌make relevant contributions ▌qualify or justify ▌deal politely with opposing views	
2. A coastal holiday photocopiable page 95		▌ask relevant questions ▌respond to others	▌make relevant contributions ▌vary contributions ▌qualify or justify ▌deal politely with opposing views ▌help the group to move forward	
3. Different coastlines for different people photocopiable pages 96–100		▌ask relevant questions ▌respond to others	▌make relevant contributions ▌vary contributions ▌deal politely with opposing views	
4. Coastal erosion catastrophe photocopiable page 101	▌use vocabulary and syntax ▌choose relevant material ▌show shape and organisation ▌speak audibly and clearly	▌ask relevant questions ▌respond to others	▌make relevant contributions ▌qualify or justify ▌deal politely with opposing views	

What is a coast?

Background information
Whether you use all of the geographical terms which have been included with this activity will clearly depend on children's previous knowledge and experience. Essentially coasts are associated with sea rather than other stretches/areas of water. Bays and peninsulas can have a coast; lakes and lochs can have a shoreline but not a coastline. The quiz provides the children with an enjoyable way of consolidating their knowledge. They need to know the answers to be able to devise the questions!

What to do
Ask the children about places they have visited recently – perhaps on holiday – and try to establish whether these places have been at the coast. Imagine that someone has recently been to Lake Windermere or Inverary (on Loch Shira) and ask if these places are on the coast. Explain that groups are now going to discuss what they think a coast is. Issue the definitions cut out from photocopiable page 94 and ask groups to sort the definitions into statements that define what a coast is and statements that do not. Alert the children to the fact that there may be more than one correct definition.

Once they have made their decision, tell the groups to check their definitions before they move on to the second part of the task. It is important that children are reassured about their responses, particularly the ones that they are unsure about. However, consider how you will do this without too much intervention in their discussion. Ensure that all the groups have numbers 3, 5 and 7 as definitions for a coast.

Next, ask the groups to put their chosen definitions of a coast to one side and focus on the other statements. Tell them to discuss what they think each statement defines. Hand out the remaining list of terms, cut out from photocopiable page 94, and ask them to match the terms to the definitions. Demonstrate how they might go about this even if they are not entirely sure of all the definitions, for example *I think I know what a loch is, so we could match this up just now. Does anyone else agree with me? An island is definitely not _____ or _____. Could it be _____? What do you think?*

Review the answers to photocopiable page 94 with the class after all the groups have finished. Test the children's understanding by making statements

Objectives
▌ To summarise and use previous knowledge to help the group move forward

▌ To accommodate different views by using particular phrases

▌ To listen to others' ideas to clarify thinking

You will need
▌ photocopiable page 94

Activity time
1 hour 30 minutes

Assessment
▌ Did the children review periodically what had been learned during their discussion to help them to clarify their ideas?

▌ To what extent were they able to accommodate different views to sort and match terms and definitions and to devise a quiz?

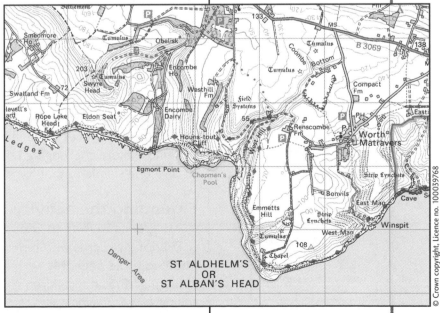

and asking questions, such as *So a loch can have a shore but not a coast. Does a bay only have a coastline?* The answers are: 1. riverbank; 2. island; 3. coast; 4. shore; 5. coast; 6. peninsula; 7. coast; 8. lake; 9. bay; 10. loch; 11. headland.

Tell the children that they are now going to use the terms and definitions to make a geography quiz for teachers, parents or older brothers and sisters. Model different question formats to the children, for example:

■ (multiple choice) *Please circle the correct answer: A bay is a _____ , _____ or _____ .*

■ (true/false) *A bay is a piece of land surrounded by water. True/false.*

■ (the first letter of a word describing a type of coast is given, with spaces counted out for the other letters) *A part of the sea filling a large-mouthed opening of land. B_ _.*

Encourage the groups to add other geographical terms and definitions to their quiz. Ask the groups to consider the order that they want to put their questions in too. Once you have offered these suggestions, leave the groups to devise their own quiz. Depending on children's ICT skills, they should be supported in putting their quiz onto the computer.

Ensure that each group's quiz is distributed and that an opportunity is provided for the other groups to read and, if necessary, correct the completed quizzes.

Simplifying the activity

■ Include only one of the definitions for a coast.
■ Remove more challenging terms/definitions, such as *peninsula*.
■ Give one simple format for the quiz design.

Extending the activity

■ Ask groups to form their own definition of a coast.
■ Do not give cards with terms for the second part of the activity on photocopiable page 94.
■ Suggest that the children sort the terms into *can have a coastline/ cannot have a coastline*.

A coastal holiday

Background information
Although dependent on children's individual experiences, this activity is likely to extend their ideas about why people go on holidays at the coast beyond 'to play in the water'. It will also alert them to the interests and needs of different groups of people.

What to do
Distribute a set of four cards copied and cut out from photocopiable page 95 (together with four blank cards) to each group and ask the children to read the four reasons suggested for people going on coastal holidays. Give the children time in their groups to discuss these and to add other reasons for going on coastal holidays on the blank cards provided. Intervene if you think groups need some prompting with ideas (for example, sailing, swimming, fishing and so on). Now ask the groups to rank each of the reasons from most popular to least popular after discussing and making predictions about each option. Direct the children to the left-hand section of photocopiable page 95 for them to record their predictions. For those finding it difficult to compromise and reach agreement you may have to offer and model some frameworks to help, such as *Do we agree… Who disagrees… Hold on before we make a final decision…*

In order for children to check their predictions about coastal holidays, suggest that groups design a questionnaire seeking the views of family and friends. (They could allow people to add a different reason for going on a coastal holiday, if it is not among their cards.)

After collation of the results, ask the children to rank the reasons in order of popularity in the section *Our findings* on the photocopiable sheet. They should then compare the ranking with their own predictions. After they have reviewed their findings, they should complete the concluding sentences underneath. Bring the class together and display each group's statements and questions, helping the children to review and speculate about the findings.

Simplifying the activity
■ Offer the children six reasons to rank in order.

Extending the activity
■ Ask the children to compare differences between the reasons children and adults choose to go on coastal holidays.

Objectives
▌ To handle disagreement and reach agreement in an appropriate manner

▌ To speculate on reasons for doing something from another perspective

You will need
▌ Photocopiable page 95

▌ Blank cards

▌ Multiple copies of groups' questionnaires

Activity time
1 hour 35 minutes

Assessment
▌ How did children handle disagreement and reach agreement? Were they able to make use of some of the language structures offered to do this?

▌ Were children able to suggest reasons for doing something from a perspective other than their own?

Different coastlines for different people

Objectives
▮ To justify decisions

▮ To maintain roles using appropriate language structures

You will need
▮ Photocopiable pages 96–100

▮ Maps with coastlines and keys to denote different features

▮ A collection of postcards and photographs with views of coastlines of the UK

Activity time
1 hour 10 minutes

Assessment
▮ Did the children justify their decisions?

▮ Did they stay in role using appropriate language?

Background information
In this activity the children role-play a scene in a travel agency between travel agents and customers requesting particular kinds of coastal holidays.

What to do
About a week before the activity, ask the children to bring in any postcards or photographs which they may have showing views of coastlines in the UK. Recap on what a coast is – that it is where the land meets the sea.

Look at the children's postcards and photographs together. Do any of them show areas they have visited? Establish that some coastlines may have a combination of bays and headlands (see photocopiable page 97 for different types of coasts that can be found in the UK).

Talk about holidays and how people may choose a particular destination because they want to be by the sea. Tell the children that if they were travel agents and customers were seeking their advice about seaside holidays, they would need to know about different kinds of coastlines and how some are more appealing than others depending on a holidaymaker's requirements. For example, a couple with young children may prefer a sandy beach to one with shingle because their children want to build sandcastles. Organise the children into groups of approximately four. Issue copies of photocopiable pages 96 and 97 and invite the children to try to match the different coastlines on the second photocopiable sheet to the travellers on the first sheet. Make sure the children understand that some travellers may be satisfied with a number of different types of coast. Encourage the children to use their own experience and any postcards with views to suggest possible locations, when filling in the final section of each box on photocopiable page 96. They can then use the maps you have prepared for them to locate areas more precisely, referring to the key.

You may want to sit with a group to model justifying opinions, using phrases such as *And the reason I think this is… Why do you say that, Martin? Why do you think that I have come to that decision? That's an interesting idea. What makes you say that?*

Undertake the next part of the activity, which involves the children in role-play, a day or so later to give them time to research coastal destinations in the UK. In preparation for the role-play, split the class into two groups: travel agents and customers. There should be about six to eight travel agents, with the rest of the children being customers.

In groups of three or four, the travel agents can plan questions that they will ask to ascertain the requirements of their customers and to help them consider possible holiday destinations. Give the children copies of photocopiable page 98 to help them with the planning of appropriate questions.

Now ask the two groups to come together to share their ideas and to negotiate a final list of six questions (see page 14 for further advice on this snowballing technique). All the agents should take note of their questions. They can then add any other questions of their own.

Photocopiable page 99 has been designed to help the children discuss appropriate language for the travel agents. You may wish to issue this to the groups to discuss on their own before taking feedback on their decisions. Or you may wish to sit with children, using the photocopiable sheet to guide their thinking.

Group the rest of the class – the travellers – into families of four or so. Ask each group to devise names and ages for themselves and discuss possible types of favourite activities on or near coasts. They should also discuss possible locations in the UK that they would like and ones that they would discount. Issue copies of photocopiable page 100 to help the children get into role and to start to consider some language features of each character.

Now ask each travel agent to sit with each family group. The agents should talk through the questions and should note the responses.

Simplifying the activity
■ Provide postcards for the children to match to each set of travellers' requirements and help the children to locate these places on the maps.

Extending the activity
■ Children could devise a slogan, of no more than ten words, for a given location with a particular type of coastline, for example *Visit Dover's White Cliffs. Not just for bluebirds!*

Coastal erosion catastrophe

Objectives

▌ To justify opinions about courses of action

▌ To listen to others' opinions and to be prepared to change one's mind

▌ To use appropriate language to help negotiate a final decision

You will need

▌ Photocopiable page 101

▌ Blank cards

▌ Photographs of coastal erosion at www.dover.gov.uk/coast/coastal-erosion.asp

Activity time

15 minutes for each part of the task

Assessment

▌ Did the children try to justify their opinions and listen to others' opinions before coming to a decision?

▌ Did they show a willingness to change their minds after hearing other opinions?

▌ Did they try to use the phrases that were modelled?

Background information

This activity deals with the human problems associated with the erosion of the coastline. Children are asked to put themselves in the position of a family whose house is built on a cliff. The cliff is eroding and the house is now in danger of falling into the sea. What are the options for the family? Pictures of coastal erosion are available on the Internet and may help to bring this issue alive to children.

What to do

Show the children the pictures of Oldstairs Bay, Kingsdown (see website address). Explain that the pictures show the coastal erosion that has taken place during that period. Discuss how the people who lived there must have felt. Ask the children why they think this happened. Introduce the idea that people cannot only increase the likelihood of erosion, they can also work to stop erosion, for example by building groynes and sea walls. Have the children seen these on any trips to the coast?

Cut out the cards from copies of photocopiable page 101, adding some blank ones for children to add their own ideas, and give a set of cards to each group together with the top half of the photocopiable sheet. Explain that on the sheet the scenario the children are to discuss is presented.

Give the children time to read through the scenario, then discuss it, as a class. Look at the cards together, stressing that they must consider each option in turn, give it a mark from one to four, listen to others' views and be prepared to change their minds about what action they should take. Tell the children that the group's decision can be a majority decision (not unanimous) but that once they have decided on the option that most agree with they will be ready to join with another group to negotiate.

Stress that many people find it hard to negotiate but that this is the point of the activity. Remind the children that changing one's mind is

Oldstairs Bay 1950

Oldstairs Bay 1999

© Dover District Council

not a sign of weakness! Write some phrases on the board that children might want to use to help them negotiate, such as *Yes, your idea sounds a bit better than mine. Well, I still like my idea but I'll go with yours because… It sounds like most people like your idea, so I'll agree to it too. How about taking this part of my idea and adding this part of Andrew's?* Tell the children that you would like groups to volunteer for you to sit with them to hear how well they listen and negotiate.

Obviously if children are to negotiate the final decision it will be necessary for the two groups to have reached different conclusions to this first part of the task. You can monitor progress of this if the whole class is in groups simultaneously. If children are undertaking this at different times in the week you will have time to pair up appropriate groups at a later date.

Simplifying the activity
■ Provide the children with articles from newspapers and the Internet about incidents of coastal erosion, then allow the children to study the cards made from photocopiable page 101 and reach a group decision about the best course of action to take.

Extending the activity
■ When the children have reached a final decision about a solution to the scenario on photocopiable page 101, encourage them to find out what happened to Scarborough's Holbeck Hall Hotel. It fell into the sea in 1993 as a result of a landslip caused by heavy rainfall saturating the dry and cracked boulder clay of the cliff.

Quiz – what is a coast?

| headland | peninsula | shore | island | lake | bay | riverbank | loch |

1. The edge of a river

2. A piece of land surrounded by water

3. A zone where land and sea meet

4. Land that skirts the sea or a large body of water

5. A border of land near sea

6. A piece of land projecting far into the sea

7. The line of the seashore

8. A large body of water entirely surrounded by land

9. A part of the sea filling a large-mouthed opening of land

10. A Scottish lake

11. A narrow area of land jutting out into a sea, lake and so on

Why do people go on coastal holidays?

| watch birds | walk | sunbathe | rock-climb |

Our predictions

1. _____
2. _____
3. _____
4. _____
5. _____
6. _____
7. _____
8. _____

Our findings

1. _____
2. _____
3. _____
4. _____
5. _____
6. _____
7. _____
8. _____

We thought that the most popular reason for going on coastal holidays would be to _____

We found out that the most popular reason for going on coastal holidays is to _____

We were therefore (surprised/not surprised) by our findings.

We thought that the least popular reason for going on coastal holidays would be to _____

We found out that the least popular reason for going on coastal holidays is to _____

We were therefore (surprised/not surprised) by our findings.

SCHOLASTIC

Different coastlines for different people

Ms Singh

Likes beach walks

Type of coast/s

Possible locations

The Campbell family

The children like to play on the beach

Type of coast/s

Possible locations

Mr Ross and Ms Quinn

Like to sunbathe

Type of coast/s

Possible locations

Mr Frame

Takes photographs of scenery

Type of coast/s

Possible locations

Ms Green

Collects shells

Type of coast/s

Possible locations

Ms Diaz

Likes to watch the waves crashing

Type of coast/s

Possible locations

Different types of coast

Headland with arches

Headland with stacks

Headland with caves

Bay with sand

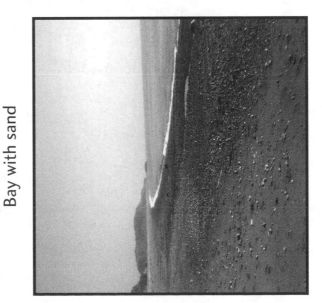

Bay with shingle

SCHOLASTIC

Travel agents' questions

▌ In your travel agency you are discussing seaside holidays in the UK with your customers. Choose four questions to ask each family to find out the type of seaside destination that would suit them.

1. Do you like seaside resorts?

2. What do you like to do when on holiday?

3. Does everyone in your family like to do the same things?

4. Are there any places in the UK that you do not want to travel to?

5. Do you have any particular UK destination in mind?

6. Which other seaside holidays have you had?

7. Why do you like seaside holidays?

8. Which is the best seaside holiday that you have had?

9. Will everyone in the family be travelling together?

10. Why do you like going on holiday?

Travel agents' phrases

z How might a travel agent greet a customer?

"Hi! You want to go on holiday, yeah?"

"Hello there. Can I help you?"

"Hiya!"

"So you like holidays? Cool!"

"Hi. Please take a seat. I'll be with you in a minute."

"How do you do."

"Yes?"

"So glad you have decided to travel with us. You won't be disappointed."

z Can you add other suitable and unsuitable greetings?

z Which of these phrases are suitable/unsuitable for a travel agent?

"I would highly recommend…"

"Your family would love…"

"Don't even think about travelling to…"

"Have you thought of…?"

"Would you consider…?"

"Why on earth are you thinking of going to…"

"You'd hate…"

"Let me offer you another idea."

z Can you add other suitable and unsuitable phrases?

z How might a travel agent finish the conversation with customers?

"Thanks for doing business with us."

"See ya!"

"You have made a wise decision."

"I wish I were coming with you."

"Have a great holiday!"

"Goodbye, I have other customers to see to."

"You won't be disappointed."

"Enjoy!"

"Bye bye."

z Can you add other suitable and unsuitable phrases?

SCHOLASTIC

Families on holiday

▌ How many adults are in your family? ☐
▌ How many children are in your family? ☐
▌ Fill in a copy of the character profile here for each member of your family.
▌ Decide who is to be each member.

Character profile

Full name	Nickname Age
Food likes	Food dislikes
TV likes	TV dislikes
Hobbies	
3 words to describe face	3 words to describe hair
3 words to describe personality	What you like to do on seaside holidays
Seaside locations in the UK that you:	
■ would like to visit	■ would not like to visit
Favourite words/phrases (you can choose a few from the list on the right and add your own)	

"Cool!"

"No way!"

"OK"

"How lovely!"

"Under no circumstances"

"Let me think, now, sounds fine to me"

"Don't know"

"Yeah, fine"

"Well..."

"Sure"

"Well now, there's a thought"

"What do you think?"

"Terrific"

"How should I know?"

"Wonderful"

"Nah!"

"Smashing"

"How interesting"

Coastal erosion catastrophe

Since you were born your family has lived in a house on the cliffs. You love your house! Your mum has just found out that the cliffs are being eroded and the house is slowly slipping down. In 20 years' time it will probably fall into the sea.

■ What should your family do? Look at the options on the cards. You can add others of your own on some blank cards. In your group talk about each option and give it a mark from 1 (not a sensible option) to 4 (a sensible option). Then decide on the one course of action you would choose.

not sensible ← 1 — 2 — 3 — 4 → sensible

Ask the council to give you another house. ☐

Do nothing. ☐

Ask the council to pay for a sea wall to be built to stop further erosion. ☐

Ask the council to pay for shoring up the house. ☐

Try to shore the house up by yourselves. ☐

Try to sell the house but don't tell anyone about the erosion. ☐

Try to sell the house but tell the people about the problem. ☐

Linked to
The National Curriculum for geography, Key Stage 2, 'An environmental issue caused by attempts to manage the environment sustainably [for example, by reducing water use]'; Scottish environmental studies 5–14 guidelines, social subjects, 'People in society'; science, 'Earth and space'

Water

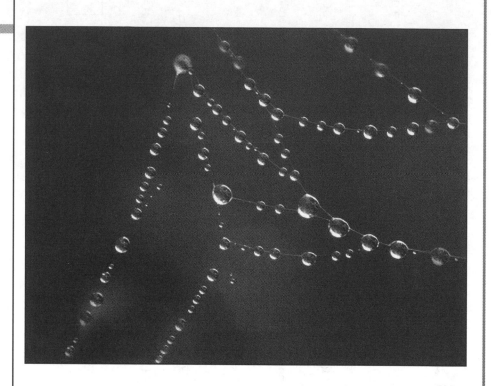

Activity	speaking	listening	group discussion	drama
1. Rain is free! photocopiable pages 110 and 111		▌ ask relevant questions ▌ respond to others	▌ make relevant contributions ▌ qualify or justify ▌ deal politely with opposing views	
2. The water is off! photocopiable page 112		▌ ask relevant questions ▌ respond to others	▌ make relevant contributions ▌ qualify or justify ▌ deal politely with opposing views ▌ sustain different roles	
3. Dripping tap photocopiable pages 113 and 114		▌ ask relevant questions ▌ respond to others	▌ make relevant contributions ▌ vary contributions ▌ deal politely with opposing views ▌ help the group to move forward	
4. Bottled water photocopiable pages 115 and 116	▌ use vocabulary and syntax ▌ choose relevant material ▌ gain and maintain interest of audience ▌ speak audibly and clearly ▌ evaluate speech	▌ ask relevant questions ▌ respond to others	▌ make relevant contributions ▌ qualify or justify ▌ deal politely with opposing views ▌ help the group to move forward	

Rain is free!

Background information
This activity could be used as an introduction to a study of water. Children may be puzzled as to why we have to pay for something that is apparently free. This task involves children considering and discussing the many different services that water companies undertake and how vital they are to a community.

What to do
Give copies of the top half of photocopiable page 110 to groups of four children, explaining that it outlines some services that a water company might provide. Ask the children to imagine that they are running a water company in a fictitious town called Milltown, and to justify each service in turn.

Now provide the children with budget cards copied and cut out from photocopiable page 111. Explain that these contain information about budget limitations (for example, £250 for maintaining water towers). Ask the children to select the services that they will focus on for the coming week; they cannot spend more than £1000, so they will not be able to choose more than three services. You can encourage them to deal politely with opposing views here by modelling sentence starters, for example *I see what you mean, Sandeep, but perhaps we could also think of... I disagree with the point that Carol is making because... Your idea sounds good but it may not work because...*

After they have made their decisions, provide the children with the events cards, one by one (copied and cut out from photocopiable page 110), to see whether they want to change their minds about how they will spend the cash.

Simplifying the activity
■ Offer the children the cards provided at the bottom of photocopiable page 110 to help them with justifying the services the water company provides.

Extending the activity
■ Encourage the children to contact their local water company for information on how the money they obtain from water charges is spent. They can then make up their own cards for the costing activity with more realistic budget figures.
■ Children could role-play a committee meeting about how to spend the week's budget.

Objectives
▌ To justify decisions
▌ To deal with opposing views

You will need
▌ Photocopiable pages 110 and 111

Activity time
1 hour 30 minutes

Assessment
▌ Were the children's justifications realistic?
▌ Did the children use modelled phrases to deal politely with opposing views about how to spend the money?

Objectives
▍ To devise group plans

▍ To co-operate to implement group plans

▍ To listen for information and note-take simultaneously

You will need
▍ Photocopiable page 112

▍ One litre bottle for each group

▍ Measuring jugs

▍ Children's own toothbrush/toothpaste

▍ Fruit for rinsing

Activity time
2 hours

Assessment
▍ Did group plans cover important aspects of the investigation?

▍ To what extent was co-operation evident during the investigation?

▍ Were the children able to listen for information and note-take simultaneously?

The water is off!

Background information
The first part of this activity involves the children in predicting how much water they think will be used up undertaking basic routines, for example brushing teeth. The second part allows them to carry out the routines themselves to find out the amount of water that is actually used.

What to do
Present the children with the announcement at the top of photocopiable page 112 from the local water board informing them that the water in their area will be turned off for 24 hours in order for essential maintenance to be done. Point out that the leaflet also includes information about how much water is used for different tasks.

Organise the children into groups. Issue a copy of the table on photocopiable page 112 to each child in each group. Ask the children to discuss their estimates for each routine – brushing teeth, washing face and so on – as a group, and to note their group estimate for each routine in the second column of the table provided.

Ask the children to plan how they will organise the undertaking of the routines. Consider providing them with leading questions to help them with their planning, for example what needs to be done; what resources are required; how will different people in the group be involved? Direct the children to carry out the routines, measuring and noting the amounts of water used. You may want the children to do this one group at a time. Or you could ask each group to undertake a different routine, then arrange a report-back session in which children make notes on their individual tables regarding the amount of water used for each routine. If you opt for the latter, ask one of the groups to present their information about how much water is used when, for example, rinsing grapes, and model how to listen to this information and take notes in the appropriate places on the table.

When the columns *Estimate* and *Amount used* have been completed, ask the children questions and comment on their findings, for example *Which estimate were you closest to? Which estimate were you furthest out on? I am surprised about the amount of water used to…*

Ask the children to look at the information they have noted on their table and to consider multiple instances of certain routines, for example at least twice a day for brushing teeth. They should then calculate a figure to fill in the column *Amount used in a day*.

Remind the children that the water company has allocated one litre of water per person per day. Ask the groups to decide whether all the routines would be possible with this amount of water. They should reach the conclusion that they will not have enough water to undertake all the routines. Ask the children to work in their groups to think of safe alternatives and/or water efficiencies for any or all of the routines (such as sharing the water or using wet wipes for hands). They should note these in the final column of the table.

Organise a report-back session during which groups offer ideas about safe alternatives, with other groups adding these ideas to their own tables.

Simplifying the activity

■ Omit the final part of the activity, which focuses on safe alternatives.

Extending the activity

■ Ask the children to prepare a short public information document or poster about how much water is used undertaking routine chores, adding suggestions about what can be done to save water during water shortages (see below).

Water shortages

Did you know?

It takes _____ of water

to _____!

Have you considered _____

_____ to save water?

Dripping tap

Objectives
▌ To reach a joint decision

▌ To help the group to move forward during a planning process

▌ To speak audibly and clearly when making presentations

You will need
▌ Photocopiable pages 113 and 114

▌ The help of a classroom assistant

▌ Various containers for holding water

Activity time
1 hour

Assessment
▌ Did the children listen well to others' opinions and modify their ideas to reach a compromise?

▌ Did they speak audibly and clearly when making a presentation of their findings?

Background information
In this activity, children are asked to predict the amount of water that might be wasted by dripping taps. They are then asked to discuss how they might find this out for themselves, how they could inform others of the wastage, and how such wastage can be prevented. Carrying out this task will help children to appreciate the amount of water that is wasted by dripping taps and to be aware of the waste of water in many public and domestic places. It should also encourage them to be alert to such wastage in their school and at home.

What to do
This activity is best carried out by groups of three children. Different groups can compare findings before jointly planning and delivering the presentation.

Write the following information on the board:
We think that a dripping tap will waste

■ less than 1 litre of water a day

■ about 1 litre of water a day

■ about 2 litres of water a day

■ about 4 litres of water a day

■ about 10 litres of water a day

■ much more than 10 litres of water a day.

Invite groups to make a guess at the amount of water wasted over a 24-hour period. Ask the groups to decide which statement they agree with the most and to write it down.

Now give the children copies of photocopiable page 113 to help them consider a practical means of measuring the amount. (You might decide to change option three to accommodate the children's attainment levels in maths.) When the groups have got started on the activity, take the opportunity to spend some time with groups who need your help in their discussions; model the type of talk that will help the group to move forward, for example *Let's talk about the least possible one first. So are we saying that option four is out? How many of us feel the same way as Sally? What are we left with now? So who could sum up what we think so far?*

When the children have decided on the best means of finding out how much water would be wasted in a day by the

dripping tap, you should discuss the practicalities with them, gently pointing out any reasons for some options being impractical.

Children will need the supervision of a classroom assistant to carry out the investigation. The classroom assistant should set the tap at a steady drip for children to investigate the amount of water that would be wasted in places that have dripping taps.

Give time for groups to observe the dripping tap over the agreed time period and to collect the water in a container. When children are finished they should measure the amount. They will now be ready to consider how they will present their findings to the rest of the class (or to another audience). Issue copies of photocopiable page 114 to help them discuss this. They will need your help in matching the means of presenting to the audience and perhaps in gathering the resources. Children may also need time to rehearse the presentation.

Simplifying the activity
■ Give the children fewer options to consider when they are working on photocopiable page 113.
■ Display the children's findings rather than asking them to prepare an oral presentation of their findings.

Extending the activity
■ Ask the children to make a poster for the school toilets, staffroom and any other places where there are taps to urge people not to leave taps dripping. The children could think of a slogan to include, perhaps using alliteration or rhyme.

Bottled water

Background information
The purpose of this activity is for children to plan a survey related to who uses bottled water, why they use it and what they use it for. Children are also encouraged to reach conclusions about who uses bottled water and why.

What to do
Direct the children's attention to the three main areas that they will be investigating when looking at the use of bottled water:
▪ Who uses bottled water?
▪ What do people use bottled water for?
▪ Why do people use bottled water?

Put these questions on display and ask the children to use them as headings for their survey form. Discuss each question in turn. For example, for question one, the children could think about people's age, gender and occupation; for question two they could think about uses such as for drinking, cooking, making tea and coffee, and making up babies' bottles; for question three they could consider health reasons, the taste of bottled water and the convenience. Give the children copies of photocopiable page 115, which has ideas for the content and layout of their survey form. Ask the children to plan the content and layout of each question in turn, examining some of the options provided. Encourage groups to add some ideas of their own. Introduce some of the language of decision-making to the children in the context of their planning, for example *Do we agree? Who disagrees? Why? Is this the best plan? Is there anything else we should consider? So this is what we are going to do.*

Suggest that the children write questions on individual pieces of paper to help them decide on a final sequence for their questions. Model how to decide on this in their groups, for example *I think this one should come after that one about _____ because... Maybe we should ask this question earlier as it lets people know...*

Support the children in using ICT to present a final version of their survey. Arrange for each group's survey to be distributed to parents and carers. (You could also send it to parents and carers of children in other classes to broaden the number of people surveyed.)

When the surveys have been distributed, completed and returned, ask the children to plan an efficient way of collating the results. For example, they could work in pairs within their group to aid the collation, with one child reading out responses and the other keeping a tally on an enlarged version of an unused survey sheet. They can then note down the most frequent responses to each question for their group. Ask each group to review their findings and to summarise their conclusions using the sentence starters provided on photocopiable page 116.

For presenting their findings to the others in the class, the notes they have made on photocopiable page 116 will provide a structure, and they should now make decisions about who will be responsible for presenting what information. Demonstrate how to present information at a pace which allows others to take notes.

Give the children time to practise their presentations taking account of the pace demonstrated. Using some of the children's findings, model how to listen and take notes, using the headings from photocopiable page 116 (*Who? What for? Why?* and *Other information*). Organise the group presentations and ask others to take notes on the photocopiable sheet during each of the group presentations.

After each group has presented their group findings, help the children to collate their class findings, using the notes they have made, and to summarise the class findings using the sentence starters provided on photocopiable page 116.

To provide a more authentic purpose for the activity, ask each group to draft and write a letter to a bottled water company (each group should write to a different company). The letter should inform the company about how they went about gathering information, outline their questions and findings, and ask the company about any market research they have undertaken and what the similarities are with their findings.

Simplifying the activity
■ Limit the amount of note-taking that the children undertake during the group presentations.
■ Collate responses from each of the group's findings yourself.
■ Provide paragraph headings/sentence starters for the letter based on the suggestions outlined above.

Extending the activity
■ Encourage the children to extend their investigation by adding a section to their survey form related to which factors influence the type of water people buy. (Or they could plan a follow-up survey for distribution to those who indicated that they use bottled water.) Factors the children could present for people to consider are taste, size of bottle, shape of bottle, nutrients, price, and type of bottle top.
■ Suggest that the children include the findings resulting from this part of the survey in their letter to the bottled water company.

Water issues

▌ You are a member of Milltown's Water Company. Here are some of the services that you provide. Justify why you need to provide each service.

Service	Why we provide it
Maintaining the reservoir	
Replacing old pipes	
Fixing burst pipes	
Treating the sewage	
Maintaining water towers	
Checking the water is clean	

People need clean water to drink or they will become ill.	Sewage needs to be treated to stop the smell and to prevent diseases.	The water towers need to work properly or the water will not flow into people's homes.	If people have burst pipes they need to be fixed straight away. The money has to be ready for this.
Dirty water spreads diseases.	Old pipes rot and break up. Little bits of metal would then be in the water.	Old lead pipes can make the water dangerous to drink.	If the reservoir springs a leak the water will flood the town.

Rain is free!

▌ The water company has £1000 to spend per week on the different services. How would you spend the cash?

Maintaining the reservoir £400	Maintaining water towers £250	Treating the sewage £400
Fixing burst pipes £350	Replacing old pipes £400	Checking the water is clean £400

▌ You have now decided how you would spend the cash for the week. During the week the following events occur. Do you want to change your mind?

Tuesday: Event 1
The water coming from the old pipes that serve the factory looks brown and has pieces of grit in it.

Thursday: Event 2
People are becoming ill in Milltown and are suspicious that there are bugs in the water.

Friday: Event 3
Passers-by have called to say the wall of the reservoir has sprung a leak.

SCHOLASTIC

The water is off!

FOR THE ATTENTION OF RESIDENTS IN THE MILLTOWN AREA

Milltown Water Company

Members of the public should note that the water will be turned off in your area for at least 24 hours to undertake essential repair work.

Milltown Water Company would like to apologise to customers for any inconvenience this might cause and for the short notice you have been given.

We will provide each member of every household with one litre of water.

Did you know that:

◆ 7.5–9.5 litres of water are used every time you flush your toilet.

◆ 80 litres of water are used when you take a bath.

◆ 35 litres of water are used when you take a shower.

◆ Using a washing machine uses 65 litres of water.

◆ Using a dishwasher uses up to 25 litres of water.

◆ Watering a garden using a garden sprinkler uses up to 540 litres of water an hour!

Source: www.water.org.uk

Routine	Estimate	Amount used	Amount used in a day	Safe alternative
Brushing teeth				
Washing face				
Having a drink				
Washing hands				
Rinsing grapes				

Photocopiable

Dripping tap

▌ How might you check if your guess is a good one? You will have to carry out an investigation, but how will you do this? Here are a few ideas to help you. Discuss each idea before moving on to the next one. Put a symbol in the second column to show what you think of the idea.

We don't think this is a good way to find out.   ✗
We think this is a good way to find out.   ✓
We might choose this way of finding out.   ?

Possible ways of finding out	What we think of this idea	Why this idea would/ would not work
1. We could ask the caretaker how much water would be wasted.		
2. We could attach a tube to a dripping tap and put the other end of the tube into a bucket and leave it for 24 hours, then measure it.		
3. We could collect the drips in a jug for 5 minutes. Then we could measure it. We could then multiply the amount by the number of 5 minutes in a day.		
4. We could stay up for 24 hours and collect all the drips.		
5. Your own idea:		

Presenting our findings

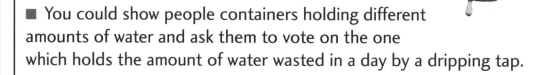

■ You will want to tell others what you have found but you don't want to bore them! So try to get your audience involved in some way.

■ You could ask people to guess how much is wasted by a dripping tap in a day, then tell them the answer.

■ You could show people containers holding different amounts of water and ask them to vote on the one which holds the amount of water wasted in a day by a dripping tap.

■ Your own idea:

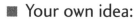

Think about:	Our notes
when you will carry this out	
what resources you will need	
what you will say to people	

Using bottled water

▌ Discuss the best way to set out the questions that you want to ask. Look at some of the suggestions here to help you to plan your survey.

> **Remember:**
> ■ people will not want to spend a lot of time writing things out
> ■ you need to ask for information politely

If you want people to write their own ideas you will need to ask an open question like *What do you use bottled water for?* or include a space for *Other reasons*. If you want people to choose from your group's ideas you will need to ask closed questions. Here is a sample survey form.

BOTTLED WATER SURVEY

Please tick the appropriate boxes.

Age	3–12 ☐	13–18 ☐	19–30 ☐
31–45 ☐	46–60 ☐	61–75 ☐	76+ ☐

Gender   male ☐   female ☐

Occupation

What do you use bottled water for?	**Why do you use bottled water?**
Drinking ☐	I think it's healthier than tap water. ☐
Cooking ☐	I prefer the taste. ☐
Brushing teeth ☐	It's convenient. ☐
Rinsing fruit/vegetables ☐	Other reason ☐ (please state)
Making tea/coffee ☐	
Babies' bottles ☐	
Other reason ☐ (please state)	

Bottled water – who and why?

Group's conclusions:

The people who use bottled water are _____

and _____.

The most common use of bottled water is to _____

_____.

The main reason for using bottled water is _____

_____.

We also found out that _____

_____

Note-taking for group presentations:

Who?	What for?	Why?	Other information

Class conclusions:

The people who use bottled water are _____

and _____.

The most common use of bottled water is to _____

_____.

The main reason for using bottled water is _____

_____.

We also found out that _____

_____

Seeds

Unit 7

Linked to
The National Curriculum for science, Key Stage 2, 'Life processes and living things – green plants; reproduction'; Scottish environmental studies 5–14 guidelines, science, 'Living things and the processes of life'

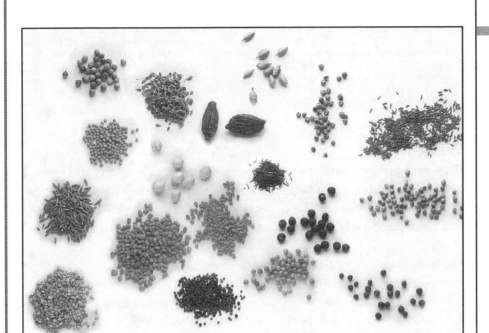

Activity	speaking	listening	group discussion	drama
1. What is a seed?		▌ask relevant questions ▌respond to others	▌make relevant contributions ▌qualify or justify ▌deal politely with opposing views ▌help the group to move forward	
2. Seed dispersal mechanisms photocopiable page 124		▌ask relevant questions ▌respond to others	▌make relevant contributions ▌qualify or justify ▌deal politely with opposing views	
3. Seeds: information gap photocopiable pages 125 and 126	▌use vocabulary and syntax ▌gain and maintain interest of audience ▌choose relevant material ▌show shape and organisation ▌speak audibly and clearly ▌evaluate speech	▌identify gist/key points ▌recall important features ▌identify language features for specific purposes		
4. Eating seeds! photocopiable pages 127 and 128		▌ask relevant questions ▌respond to others	▌make relevant contributions ▌qualify or justify ▌deal politely with opposing views ▌help the group to move forward	

What is a seed?

Objectives
❚ To achieve compromise where necessary

❚ To listen to others' ideas and relate this to previous discussions

❚ To modify opinions in light of new information

You will need
❚ A collection of seeds and non-seeds (see suggestions)

Activity time
45 minutes

Assessment
❚ How did children manage to compromise?

❚ To what extent were children able to listen to others' ideas and relate this to previous discussions?

❚ How willing were children to modify their opinions in light of new information?

Background information
This activity should help extend children's knowledge about the different sizes, shapes and colours of seeds. Vocabulary such as *seed, stone, kernel* and *pip* will be reinforced through this work. The conclusions reached should emphasise that the size of a seed need not be proportional to the size of the 'fruit'. A key point to establish is that we can tell if something is a seed if we plant it and it grows. However, we can plant something which is a seed but it may not grow for a variety of reasons, for example because it has been damaged or because conditions are not right for germination.

What to do
Give each group a similar collection which includes a variety of seeds, and items which are not seeds (but some of which may be mistaken for seeds). Suggestions for the collections are outlined below. An asterisk has been placed next to those items which are seeds, or contain seeds.

*peppercorns   *mango stone   *peach stone   *orange pips   *sesame seeds
*poppy seeds   *sunflower seeds   *apple pips   *variety of flower seeds
*variety of vegetable seeds   empty pine cones   acorn cups
cake decorations   small sweets   small plastic items

Ask the groups to sort the items in their collection under three headings:
■ seeds
■ not seeds
■ can't tell.

Give the children sufficient time to work on this as it will allow them to share their experiences and rely on each other's knowledge. While

some of the items will be quite straightforward for children to sort, others may be trickier and there will be different opinions in the group about them.

Encourage the children to listen to others' reasons for why they think an item is a seed or not and provide the children with some opening phrases to help them to compromise, such as *Why don't we put it in the 'can't tell' set just now and talk about it again later?* Or *I am not sure that I agree but I'll wait and hear some other ideas before I make up my mind.*

After approximately 20 minutes, regroup the children to envoy their findings and to seek clarification of ideas (see page 14 for guidance on envoying). Each envoy should go to another group to ask the questions:

- *What does your group have in the 'seeds' set?*
- *What has your group decided are not seeds?*
- *What has your group put into the 'can't tell' set?*

For the third question, the envoy may be able to offer some information from his or her group's discussion. Or the envoy may gain further information about items in the collection which his or her group found difficult to classify.

Allow ten minutes for envoys to report back to their groups. If there are any discrepancies between the results of the group visited and the envoy's own group, this should provide the children with a further opportunity to make changes to the seeds' classification, if necessary. Explain to them that they must decide which ideas from the envoying they will accept and which they might want to seek further clarification about.

Reassure the children that changing their opinion based on additional information is a positive attribute and does not constitute a climbdown. Help them to handle modifying their opinions by providing opening phrases, such as *I thought it was a seed because… but now that I have heard other ideas I think it is probably not a seed* and *Most people think it is not a seed and so that may be right, but I still think it could be a seed because…*

Work with the children on any items remaining in the *can't tell* set to determine ways in which they can establish whether these items are seeds or not (see Background information).

Simplifying the activity
■ Put in more obvious non-seed items into the children's collections such as paper clips and pencil shavings.

Extending the activity
■ Ask the children to sort the *seeds* set further into *only one seed per fruit* and *more than one seed per fruit*.
■ Plant those items that groups think are seeds (and that actually are seeds). For seeds that do not grow, it will reinforce the idea that non-growth does not mean that the item was not a seed.

Seed dispersal mechanisms

Background information
Plants have developed a number of ways in which their seeds can be dispersed. This activity provides a means of children deepening their understanding of which ways are used effectively by which types of seeds and why.

Objectives
▌ To sort ideas, looking for consensus in the decision-making process

▌ To devise group plans and use the language of decision-making

You will need
▌ Photocopiable page 124

▌ Different types of plants/seeds (optional)

Activity time
2 hours

Assessment
▌ Was a consensus reached after children listened to others' views?

▌ How successfully did groups allocate tasks and decide on timescales for the completion of their booklet?

What to do

Copy and cut out the different sections of the table on photocopiable page 124, mixing them up and giving one set to each group. In order to familiarise the children with the names and range of seed dispersal mechanisms, ask each group to match the names to the different ways of seed dispersal. Check each group's definitions. (The answers are as they have been ordered on the photocopiable sheet.)

Next, ask the groups to look at the pictures of different seeds on photocopiable page 124. (Or you could provide real specimens instead, if you can obtain them, to help children gain a deeper understanding of seed dispersal mechanisms. You may wish to substitute those suggested for some local plants/seeds.) Encourage the groups to spend some time discussing how each seed might be dispersed. The children should then match the pictures to the names and seed dispersal mechanisms they have previously put together, writing the names of the seeds under the dispersal mechanisms. The answers are:

Seed dispersal mechanisms	Types of seeds
bouncers and rollers	acorn, horse chestnut
parachutes	dandelion, thistle
helicopters	sycamore, ash
pepper pots	poppy
edibles	strawberry, blackberry
hookers and stickers	burdock, herb bennet
splitters	laburnum

Some children may be unfamiliar with many of the seeds. Encourage them to speculate based on their observations and through listening to others' ideas. Model how to go about this, for example *I haven't seen a seed like this but I think it could be a splitter because…* and *I wasn't sure about this seed, but _____ has just pointed out that it has a _____, so I agree with her that it could be a hooker.* Help them to get into the routine of ascertaining the extent of agreement before making a final decision about each seed by suggesting that they use phrases such as *So we are all agreed that…* and *Does anyone think that this should go in a different set?*

Each group should now use the dispersal mechanisms, the definitions and the seed pictures to compile a simple information booklet. Demonstrate how decisions might be aided by the use of a simple timetable including things to do; who will work on different aspects; how long each part should take. Show the children how to volunteer for tasks in a way which does not preclude others, for example *I would like to work on the cover, would anyone like to work with me? I think I am better at _____ than _____ but if someone could show me how to…*

After important group decisions have been made related to the cover and layout, suggest that pairs work together on agreed pages. Encourage the children to annotate the pictures provided.

Consider a suitable audience to whom the children can present their books. Perhaps groups from another class would be interested in looking at them.

Simplifying the activity
■ Offer only one type of seed for each dispersal mechanism.

Extending the activity
■ Encourage the children to introduce other seeds for sorting related to seed dispersal.
■ Children may like to investigate seeds which might be dispersed by more than one mechanism, for example acorns.

Seeds: information gap

Objectives
▐ To sustain the interest of an audience during a presentation

▐ To ask relevant questions of the presenters

▐ To listen attentively and to take notes during a presentation

You will need
▐ Photocopiable pages 125 and 126

▐ Books about seeds

▐ A selection of seeds (optional)

Activity time
1 hour 40 minutes; 10 minutes per presentation and conclusion

Assessment
▐ Were visual aids used to sustain the interest of the audience?

▐ Did the audience listen and respond by asking appropriate questions?

▐ Did children's notes reflect their ability to listen for salient points?

Background information
In this activity children find out information about different seeds, then use their notes to frame a presentation of their facts to other groups. They do not disclose the name of the seed they are presenting (there is an information gap!). As children listen to the presentations, they make notes in a table before coming to a decision about the name of the seed being presented.

What to do
Issue each group of children with a card that has the name of a different seed on it. You could include *acorn, melon seed, peach stone, peppercorn, beech nut, pine nut, mango stone*. (Provide real seeds, if you have them.) Tell the children that they have to find out particular information about their seed, then present it to the class. The class then have to guess what each group's seed is. Distribute copies of photocopiable page 125 and tell each group which letter their seed is. Provide books (and/or access to the Internet) for children to research each aspect listed along the top row of the table on the sheet.

After they have all the information required, ask each group to plan a three-minute presentation, perhaps using two or three visual aids to help keep the audience interested. Children can use photocopiable page 126 to help them plan their presentation. (You may want to arrange for all the presentations to take place on the same day. If you think that this would be too onerous for your class, you could spread them over a number of days.)

During the presentations the audience should takes notes, writing in the table on photocopiable page 125. Remind the children that taking notes will help them listen carefully to the important points of the presentations and that they can use abbreviations. You may want to demonstrate this on the board.

At the end of each presentation allow the audience to ask the presenters a total of three questions. Each child should then make a guess before coming together with their group to reach a final decision. The presenting group should listen to the guesses, then reveal the answer.

Simplifying the activity
■ Omit the presentations and ask groups to envoy (see page 14) to find out information from other groups before making their guesses.

Extending the activity
■ Children could devise some or all of their own headings for the information table on photocopiable page 125.

Eating seeds!

Background information
It would be preferable for children to have undertaken the previous tasks in this unit before doing this activity as they will then be able to make use of the knowledge they have gained. This activity involves children planning and carrying out a survey to find out what sorts of seeds and nuts people like to eat. They then make their own seed/nut snack for sale in the school or class tuck shop, having reached agreement about a name for the snack. Warning: for this activity it is important that you are aware of any children who suffer from nut allergies. Children buying food containing nuts must first seek permission from parents and carers.

What to do

Tell the children that they will shortly be making a snack to sell in the class/school tuck shop. Show them a variety of commercial seed/nut snacks. Ask them to examine these carefully. Can they identify all the seeds and nuts? You might want to draw their attention to the list of ingredients on the packaging. Encourage them to use the table they completed in the previous activity (see photocopiable page 125) to help them identify different ingredients that are nuts or seeds.

Provide each group with a selection of edible seeds and nuts, together with some small blank cards. Ask the children to identify the seeds and nuts, using reference books, if necessary. They should place any seeds they cannot categorise in a group called *Unknown*.

Once the children have identified as many nuts and seeds as possible, discuss with them the combinations of seeds/nuts they would choose if they were devising a new snack. Suggest that they carry out a survey to find out what sort of nuts people like to eat, and distribute copies of photocopiable page 127 to help them with their planning.

After carrying out the survey, the children should make up little bags of the most popular seeds/nuts. Discuss with them what each bag should weigh and what the price should be. For a name for their snack, photocopiable page 128 offers ideas.

Remind the children that sometimes it is important to be prepared to change one's mind as a result of listening to others' points of view. Model phrases that may be useful, such as *Yes, your name for the snack sounds much better than mine* or *I did think I would like my name best, but I'll go with that name.*

Simplifying the activity

■ Simply take a class vote for the name of the snack.

Extending the activity

■ The children could undertake market research before deciding on possible names for the snack.
■ They could make seed cake for different birds according to what their research tells them about different birds' likes and dislikes.

Objectives
▌ To negotiate the best means of carrying out a survey

▌ To come to a majority decision

You will need
▌ Photocopiable pages 127 and 128

▌ A variety of seed and/or nut snacks, for example sesame seed bars, peanut brittle bars

▌ Magnifying glasses

▌ A variety of seeds and nuts (edible)

▌ Small paper or plastic bags

▌ Small blank cards

▌ Reference books

Activity time
1 hour 30 minutes

Assessment
▌ Did some children refuse to change their minds during the decision-making process?

▌ Did some children agree too readily to others' views without justifying their own viewpoint first?

Seed dispersal

■ Match the names of the different types of seed to the mechanisms for dispersal.

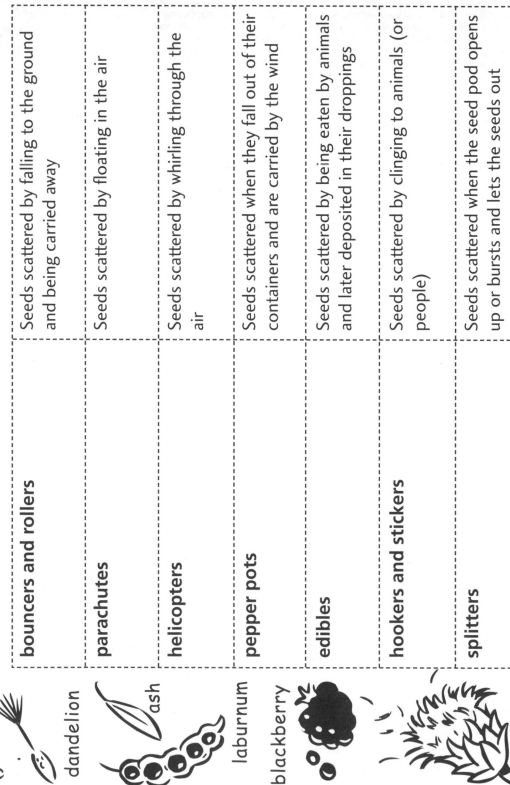

bouncers and rollers	Seeds scattered by falling to the ground and being carried away
parachutes	Seeds scattered by floating in the air
helicopters	Seeds scattered by whirling through the air
pepper pots	Seeds scattered when they fall out of their containers and are carried by the wind
edibles	Seeds scattered by being eaten by animals and later deposited in their droppings
hookers and stickers	Seeds scattered by clinging to animals (or people)
splitters	Seeds scattered when the seed pod opens up or bursts and lets the seeds out

burdock

sycamore

horse chesnut

poppy

herb bennet

strawberry

acorn

dandelion

ash

laburnum

blackberry

thistle

What seed is it?

Names of the seeds our class has been investigating:

Seed	Colour and size	Shape and texture	Conditions for germination	Countries where it grows naturally	Rate of growth	Can product be eaten?	Any other interesting fact	Our guess
A								
B								
C								
D								
E								

■ SCHOLASTIC

Planning our presentation

▌ Look at the headings on the table you have been given. Decide on the order in which you will present your findings to the class. Add 1, 2, 3 and so on to the top row of the table.

▌ Now plan a sentence for each heading.

▌ Read the sentences aloud. Can you link some sentences together?

▌ Decide where the best two or three opportunities are for pictures, photos, maps or other images to be shown to the class.

▌ Who will show the images? How? Just hold them up? Use the overhead projector?

▌ Decide who will present. Should one person do it? Should each of you present a part? Should just two present?

Seed/nut survey

The total number of seeds/nuts that we will use in our snack = ☐ .

We will therefore choose the top ☐ seeds/nuts from our survey.

Questions	Decisions	What we will need
How many seeds/nuts should we offer people?		
Which seeds/nuts should we offer people?		
Should we let people taste each seed/nut?		
How should we record the one they like best?		
Should we record any that people really hate/ are allergic to?		
How many people should we ask?		
(Your own question)		
(Your own question)		

■SCHOLASTIC

Name that snack

▌ Here are some possible names for your seed/nut snack. Your group can add other names of your own. Tick one column for each snack.

Name	Maybe	Never!
Our Seed/nut Snack		
Snacko		
Get Cracking!		
Crunch!		
Bags of Crunch		
Bags of Health		
Healthy Crunch		
Nibbles		
Bags of Nibbles		
Nifty Nibbles		
Nuts About Seeds		

▌ Now look at all the names that your group decided were 'maybe'. If there is more than one of these, your group will have to come to a decision. Discuss how you can do this fairly. Some people may have to change their minds! Come to a majority decision.

Your group's decision

Viruses and bacteria

Linked to
The National Curriculum for science, Key Stage 2, 'Life processes and living things – living things in their environment; micro-organisms';
Scottish environmental studies 5–14 guidelines, science, 'Living things and the processes of life'

Activity	speaking	listening	group discussion	drama
1. Helpful or harmful? photocopiable pages 134 and 135		▌ ask relevant questions ▌ respond to others	▌ make relevant contributions ▌ qualify or justify ▌ deal politely with opposing views	
2. Coughs & sneezes		▌ ask relevant questions ▌ respond to others	▌ make relevant contributions ▌ qualify or justify ▌ sustain different roles ▌ deal politely with opposing views ▌ help the group to move forward ▌ vary contributions	
3. Hot-seating Pasteur photocopiable page 136	▌ speak audibly and clearly	▌ ask relevant questions ▌ respond to others	▌ make relevant contributions ▌ qualify or justify ▌ deal politely with opposing views	▌ explore character and issues ▌ use character, action, narrative to convey ideas

Helpful or harmful?

Objectives
❚ To sort ideas based on information provided

❚ To reach conclusions from the sorted information

You will need
❚ Photocopiable pages 134 and 135

❚ Enlarged Carroll diagram

❚ Reference books

Activity time
45 minutes

Assessment
❚ Did the children use and refer to the information provided to sort ideas?

❚ Were they able to reach conclusions from the sorted information?

Background information
This activity should extend children's knowledge about viruses and bacteria before they undertake more extensive work in this context. The passage provided includes some basic information regarding bacteria and viruses. However, children should be directed to other sources to increase their understanding. Key points to establish are that most bacteria are harmless (and some of them can be useful), whereas viruses are harmful; a bacterium is alive, while a virus is dead and contains the code for replication when it infects a cell. People do not take antibiotics for viruses.

What to do
Give the children time to read the information on viruses and bacteria on photocopiable page 134. Revise how to complete and interpret a Carroll diagram. Put the children into groups of four and ask them to sort cards (copied and cut out from an enlarged copy of photocopiable page 135) onto a Carroll diagram (see below left). The children should use reference books and the information from photocopiable page 134 to help them. Model how to discuss and confirm ideas, for example *I think _____ is a virus. Can anyone see where it says that? Some of us think _____ can be helpful, but some of us think it can't. Let's look at the bit that tells us about _____ again to see if we can agree.*

Encourage the children to add other examples to their diagrams of where bacteria and viruses can be harmful or helpful, from information gathered from wider reading and research.

Write the following sentences on the board: *Bacteria are always/are often/are never helpful. Viruses are always/are often/are never helpful.* Ask the children to write underneath their Carroll diagram the version of each sentence that they think is correct. They should do this after consultation with the rest of the group. Offer questions that they could ask themselves, such as *What can we say about the set in the top right-hand part of the diagram? If we have not placed many cards in the bottom left-hand part of the diagram what might this tell us?* Consolidate the conclusions groups have made.

	Bacteria	Viruses
Harmful		
Can be helpful		

Simplifying the activity
■ Suggest that the children sort the cards on photocopiable page 135 into *Bacteria* and *Viruses* without further subdividing them into *Harmful* and *Can be helpful*.

■ Allow the children to work in pairs rather than groups of four.

Extending the activity
■ Add to the number of illnesses given on cards and ask the groups to research these more widely.

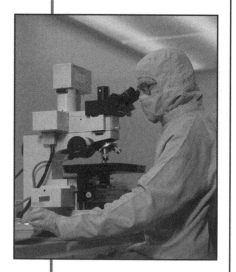

Coughs & sneezes

Background information
This activity helps children to explore the means by which viruses and bacteria are spread. (If the children have completed the previous activity, they will have been provided with valuable background information.) You may wish to visit www.netdoctor.co.uk before starting the activity.

What to do

Invite the children to tell you about any ailments and diseases they have had. (This needs to be done sensitively.) About a week before the activity, you could ask the children to construct their own questionnaire to take home to parents and carers, asking if children have suffered from measles, influenza, colds, chickenpox, rubella, diarrhoea, mumps, salmonella and so on. The questionnaire could also include questions about diseases they have been immunised against. (Make sure that parents and carers are happy to disclose information which they may consider to be confidential.)

After the discussion, and receipt of completed questionnaires, collate on the board the children's lists of diseases. Explain that we can be immunised against some viruses. Ask why no one has been immunised against diarrhoea or salmonella. What might have caused these diseases? Explain that they are caused by bacteria and that bacteria is spread by touching or through water droplets in the air.

Assign each group a disease from the class list caused by either bacteria or a virus and inform them that they will be designing a poster for the doctor's surgery/teachers' staffroom/children's toilets/school kitchen which tells people how the disease is spread and how to avoid catching it. In their groups, the children must decide on the information they will include in their poster and how it will look. Provide them with appropriate leaflets, posters and books on viruses and bacteria. Offer them a framework for the poster (see right).

Some children may need you to sit with them to encourage them to explain and justify their decisions about the poster, for example *Jade thinks that one of the colours should be dark and I agree. Let me tell you why... Why do you think that the slogan should be at the top of the page, Maria? If the image you want to add is scary how might people react to it?*

Simplifying the activity

◼ When working on their posters, provide the children with slogans from which to choose, for example (for colds) *Catch That Virus In A Hanky! Keep Sneezes To Yourself! Sneezes Spread Diseases: Use a Hanky!*

Extending the activity

◼ Set conditions for the design and content of the poster, such as no more than 15 words; no more than three colours; use alliteration, personification or rhyme.

Objectives
◼ To use appropriate phrases to justify opinions

◼ To offer suggestions which adhere to given criteria

You will need
◼ Leaflets and posters from a local doctor's surgery regarding diseases such as measles, influenza, colds, chickenpox, rubella, diarrhoea, mumps and salmonella

◼ Children's information books about diseases

Activity time
1 hour

Assessment
◼ Did the children offer suggestions which conformed to given criteria?

◼ Did they attempt to use modelled phrases to justify their opinions?

Our disease is

_____

It is caused by a virus ☐
bacteria ☐ .

The symptoms are

_____ .

It is spread by

_____ .

The best way to avoid catching it is by

_____ .

Hot-seating Pasteur

Background information
This activity gives children the opportunity to research a few basic facts about Pasteur's life and work. There are many websites available, including ones with photographs or portraits of Pasteur such as www.lucidcafe.com/lucidcafe/library/95dec/pasteur.html and www.bbc.co.uk/education/medicine/nonint/indust/dt/indtbi4.shtml. In this activity, children take on the role of interviewer and use the information they have researched to pose questions; these are directed to a child who has assumed the role of Pasteur. Before deciding who should role-play Pasteur, groups of children should be given the opportunity to determine the answers to the questions that have been posed.

What to do

Ask pairs of children to undertake research on a given aspect of Pasteur's life or work. Select a different card copied and cut out from photocopiable 136 to give to each pair and allow the children time to research their topic. (You may want to leave a day or two between issuing the topic and the next part of the activity. This will give children time to absorb and to explore the information a little more.)

Ask the pairs of children to decide on the three most interesting things they have found out about the aspect of Pasteur's life they have researched. Now ask each pair of children to join with another two pairs to form a group of six. This will be their interview group. Provide the children with copies of the second half of photocopiable page 136 to negotiate which questions they will ask and to plan the interview.

After the group has decided upon their questions and the order in which they will be asked, they should give these to another group – this group should undertake their own research to find out the answers.

At a later date the actual interview should take place. Ask the interview groups to come together, and choose one child to be Pasteur. In order to involve as many children as possible, consider having a chairperson with a panel of interviewees, rather like *Question Time*, and to give other children in the audience an opportunity to ask questions (allow interviewers a chance to rehearse beforehand). Pasteur may also have a team of scientists to help him answer the questions. This team will need to see the questions before the hot-seating in order to prepare not only the answers but the style of language that they will use. You may wish to model phrases such as *That is indeed an interesting question. Let me try to answer your question by referring to… It is my belief that… Yes, my work on pasteurisation has been applauded by many. Allow me to explain a little about it… Thank you for remembering about my work on… You are very kind to praise my work on… Your question is interesting and one I am asked frequently. Let me begin to answer it by saying…*

Point out to the children that there may be some disparity between the 'facts' that some groups have gathered and the 'facts' that others have. The issue of reliability of historical evidence should be explored so that children are not dismayed by 'wrong' responses from Pasteur! Encourage the children to speculate if they cannot find the answers to the questions posed. However, this must be divulged at the end of the hot-seating so that misconceptions are not nurtured.

Simplifying the activity
■ Give questions and answers for the children to choose from, so that they don't have to draw up their own based on research.

Extending the activity
■ Allow the children to work in small groups, each group making a video of their own interviews.

Louis Pasteur

Charles Pfizer & Co., Inc. via Soda

Helpful or harmful?

▌ Read this information, then use it to work in your group to sort the cards onto the Carroll diagram you have been given.

Bacteria are very small living things. Some are helpful to us and some are not. For instance, there are bacteria in the digestive system which help to break down our food. Helpful bacteria also live in our throats, noses and skin. In fact, bacteria are everywhere – in the air, in food, in soil and in water. Unhelpful bacteria can cause disease and even those bacteria in the gut and the skin can become harmful if they end up in the wrong place in the body.

Viruses are much much smaller than bacteria. They can enter our bodies in various ways. We can breathe them in and they can get in through cuts and scrapes. Viruses are almost always harmful. They invade our body cells and the effects are spread throughout the body.

In a non-medical sense, bacteria can be useful in that they are used in the manufacture of yoghurt and cheese. Also some bacteria can be used to fight and destroy other harmful bacteria; these are known as antibiotics.

Bacteria and viruses are so small that we cannot normally see them. However, we must remember how important it is to wash our hands before eating, when handling food and after using the toilet.

> Examples of diseases caused by bacteria: tuberculosis, food poisoning, diphtheria, leprosy and typhoid.

> Examples of diseases caused by viruses: flu, chickenpox, cold sores, mumps, measles, AIDS and colds.

SCHOLASTIC

Bacteria or virus?

Measles

Leprosy

Antibiotics

Smallpox

Common cold

Mumps

Typhoid

Influenza

Herpes (cold sores)

Tuberculosis

AIDS

Yoghurt and cheese

SCHOLASTIC

Hot-seating Pasteur

Pasteur's home town	Pasteur's main achievements related to viruses
Pasteur's timeline	Pasteur's main achievements related to vaccines
Pasteur's quotes	The process of pasteurisation
Pasteur's main achievements related to hospital practices	Other:

▍ These question starters may help you:

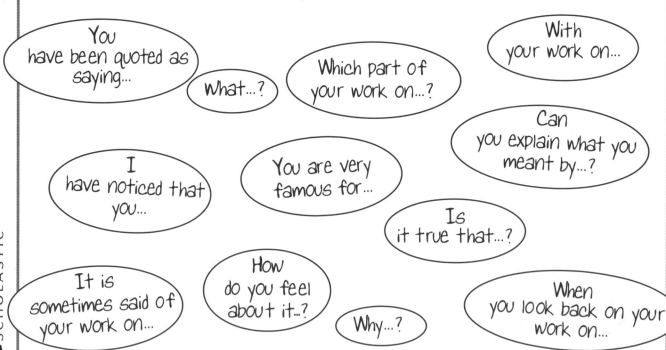

Photocopiable

Isabel

Linked to
The National Literacy Strategy *Framework for Teaching*, 'Poetry by long-established authors', 'Humorous poetry' and 'Performance poetry'; Scottish English language 5–14 guidelines, 'Reading to reflect on the writer's ideas and craft', 'Talking about texts'

Activity	speaking	listening	group discussion	drama
1. What did Isabel do? photocopiable pages 143 and 144		▌identify gist/key points ▌recall important features ▌identify language features for specific purposes	▌make relevant contributions ▌qualify or justify ▌deal politely with opposing views	
2. Isabel and the doctor photocopiable page 143	▌speak audibly and clearly ▌show shape and organisation ▌use vocabulary and syntax	▌identify gist/key points ▌recall important features ▌ask relevant questions	▌make relevant contributions ▌qualify or justify ▌deal politely with opposing views	
3. Dramatising the adventures photocopiable page 143		▌ask relevant questions ▌respond to others	▌make relevant contributions ▌vary contributions ▌deal politely with opposing views ▌help the group to move forward	▌create, adapt, sustain different roles ▌use character, action, narrative to convey ideas ▌explore characters and issues ▌evaluate contributions

What did Isabel do?

Objectives
▌ To predict possible outcomes and consequences through discussion

▌ To listen to a poem and evaluate the effectiveness of it

You will need
▌ Photocopiable pages 143 and 144

Activity time
1 hour

Assessment
▌ Were the children's predictions about outcomes and consequences based on the discussion of the text?

▌ Could they evaluate the most effective rhyme and rhythm in the poem?

Background information
The activities in this unit are based on 'Adventures of Isabel', a popular poem by the American humorist poet, Ogden Nash. Most people find this poem irresistible; its rhymes are clever, its narrative is amusing and the refrain is exceptionally memorable. You can find information about Ogden Nash at www.kyrene.k12.az.us/schools/brisas/sunda/poets/nash.htm, which the children may find interesting. If you are unfamiliar with the poem, it might be helpful to rehearse a recitation of it before examining it with the class. Note that as this activity relies on an element of prediction and surprise, it should be undertaken before any of the following activities in this unit.

What to do
Read the first stanza of Ogden Nash's poem on photocopiable page 143 to the children. Establish that although particular characters set out to frighten Isabel and cause her harm, she manages to turn the tables on them, for example rather than the bear eating Isabel, Isabel eats the bear. Explain difficult vocabulary such as *zwieback* (a teething rusk, originally from Germany), *rancour* and *concocter*.

Display an enlarged copy of the poem. Organise the children into groups and show them the other three stanzas but with the last two lines of each stanza hidden. Ask the children to read each stanza and to predict what Isabel does to the character each time. Encourage them to support their predictions with evidence from the text. Once they have reached a group decision, they should record their prediction and justification for each stanza in the first section of photocopiable page 144.

Before revealing what Isabel did do to each character, draw the children's attention to the second part of photocopiable page 144, where the penultimate line of each stanza has been given. Identify the rhyming pattern of the first stanza with the children (*hair up; bear up*) and confirm that the following stanzas are structured in the same way. Ask the groups to write a final rhyming line for each stanza based on their ideas about what they think will happen to each character. Encourage the groups to note down and play about with as many suggestions as possible for each stanza until they reach agreement on the line that has the best rhyme with the line given. Suggest that the children first make a list of rhyming words, if necessary.

Gather the class together once the groups have written a final line for the second, third and fourth stanzas. Working on one stanza at a time, collate each group's final line. First, reveal the poet's final line and establish whether their predictions were correct. Second, compare their final lines with that of the poet's. Ask the children which version they prefer and why. Start this process off by offering your own opinion, for example *It is hard to get a rhyme for 'rancour'. Ogden Nash does this well by splitting the two syllables into two words; Fiona's group have been clever by using their idea about…; I think I prefer _____, because… but I also like _____ because…*

Simplifying the activity
■ Give the children the first part of the final line when they are creating their own final line of the second, third and fourth stanzas of the poem.

Extending the activity
■ Ask the children to develop their final line of each stanza by refining the rhythm of the line.
■ Ask the groups to speculate about how other characters or creatures might try to frighten Isabel and to consider what she might do to them. The scenarios could involve an octopus, an alien, a troll or a vulture, for example.

Isabel and the doctor

Objectives
▮ To use texts to back up assertions during group discussions

▮ To structure a presentation logically, using appropriate opening phrases

You will need
▮ Photocopiable page 143

Activity time
50 minutes, then approximately 3 minutes per presentation

Assessment
▮ Did the children vary their opening phrases when presenting?

▮ Did they use only the phrases given or did they construct their own?

▮ Were the presentations constructed logically?

Background information
The fate of the doctor in the last stanza of the poem 'Adventures of Isabel' (see photocopiable page 143) is not as clear as it is for the characters she met in previous stanzas. In this activity the children have to decide in their groups what they think the most likely outcome was and are encouraged to use the text to back up their assertions.

What to do
Divide the children into groups of approximately four. Issue each group with a copy of the poem on photocopiable page 143 and ask them to re-read the last stanza. Explain that they are going to decide on the fate of the doctor by looking at various options. Write the following sentences on the board.

■ She magically cured him of an illness.

■ She gave him medicine to cure him.

■ She poisoned him.

■ She made him disappear.

■ She killed him.

Encourage the children to use evidence from the poem to substantiate their ideas about what happened to the doctor. How was he *calmly cured*? Are there any lines that they can quote from other stanzas to justify their opinions?

Once each group has decided on the doctor's fate, ask them to present their findings to other groups. They should try to structure their presentation by using different opening phrases for each stage of their decision-making, such as *When we first looked at option one... The next option... When we looked at option three...* Write some phrases on the board and encourage the children to add others of their own. They can then choose which ones to incorporate into the planning of their presentations. Remind them to draw upon the text when justifying their opinions, quoting directly from the poem.

Simplifying the activity
■ Omit the presentations and, following a discussion of the possibilities regarding the fate of the doctor, simply take a class vote on the most probable outcome.

Extending the activity
■ It might be fun to ask the children to undertake this rather like presenting a court case, using language such as *If it pleases the court... Ladies and Gentlemen of the jury, I put it to you that... My lud, and furthermore we believe that on that fateful day, Isabel...*

Dramatising the adventures

Background information
This activity can be carried out after the poem (see photocopiable page 143) has been read several times by the children and they are very familiar with it. The focus in this activity is on demonstrating the importance of how a poem is presented and how variations in pitch and pace, for example, in a performance of the poem can affect the understanding and enjoyment of it.

What to do
Distribute a copy of the poem on photocopiable page 143 to each child. Put the children into groups, assigning each group a different stanza of the poem. Ask the groups to discuss how different lines, phrases and words might be read aloud. At this stage, make sure that the children remain focused on how the lines should be read; explain that the role of Isabel will be explored later.

Remind the children of the effects of pitch and pace, and how they enunciate their words. Draw their attention to any important elements that have been looked at during earlier readings, and encourage them to experiment and to make suggestions about how they will read the poem, for example *I think the refrain should be read very slowly to show that Isabel wasn't in a hurry; We've tried saying that line loudly, what about saying it more quietly, but with a frightening look too?* Ask the children to annotate the poem to indicate how particular lines, words or phrases should be read. Build up their confidence in making changes to their notes if a more effective idea has been suggested by a member of their group.

Now ask the groups to consider how they think the character of Isabel should be portrayed. Isabel doesn't speak in the poem but we learn about her through what the poet tells us. We know, for example, that Isabel was not alarmed by each of her encounters with different characters. Encourage the children to demonstrate gestures, movements and expressions that might indicate to an audience Isabel's lack of concern about the dangers that might befall her (she didn't *worry, scream or scurry*). For example, they may want to clasp their hands behind their back and swing from side to side, gazing skywards, looking bored. Encourage the children to try out different combinations of ideas before making any group decisions.

Objectives
▌ To present a poem aloud, using narrator, chorus and different voices

▌ To explore ways of conveying character through gesture, movement and facial expression

▌ To reflect on alternative presentations

You will need
▌ Photocopiable page 143

Activity time
1 hour 10 minutes

Assessment
▌ How effectively were the children able to present the poem aloud using a narrator, chorus and different voices?

▌ Were they able to convey character through gesture, movement and facial expression?

▌ Were children able to reflect on alternative presentations in a constructive manner?

When the children have completed their planning, allocate the following parts for each stanza:

- a narrator
- the character Isabel met
- Isabel
- the chorus (who should speak the refrain *Isabel, Isabel, didn't worry, Isabel didn't scream or scurry*).

You may want children themselves to decide who is going to take these parts within their group. If so, explain that they should indicate on the left-hand side of the poem the names of children who will be performing each part. Give the children ten minutes to practise the separate parts of the stanza on which they are working, using the agreed and noted directions. Then ask them to run through their performance of the complete stanza.

Gather the class together and ask each group to present their stanza. This presentation should be undertaken at least twice. For the initial presentation the children should listen, watch and enjoy the performance of each stanza. During the repeat performance they should make brief notes beside each stanza in relation to how parts were presented. This will be useful during the reflection phase. Model how to offer constructive comments about the presentation of each stanza, for example *I thought Kashif's group managed to keep a nice rhythm during the refrain; David and Daniel spoke very clearly when they were narrating; Nicola and Joanna used very similar movements for the part of Isabel, but their gestures were quite different.*

To conclude the activity, talk with the children about how the performance of the poem has highlighted different features of it.

Simplifying the activity

- Provide more direction about how the poem should be read and how Isabel's part might be 'mimed' in a performance of the poem.
- Do not ask the children to make notes during each group's performance.

Extending the activity

- Build in a break between practice and performance for the children to memorise their lines, perhaps as part of their homework.
- Give groups an opportunity to make simple props to enhance the performance, for example a witch's hat.
- Provide a wider audience for the performance, for example another class.
- Encourage the children to experiment with different ways of splitting the poem up for reading aloud, for example would more choral reading be effective?

Adventures of Isabel

1 Isabel met an enormous bear,
Isabel, Isabel, didn't care;
The bear was hungry, the bear was ravenous,
The bear's big mouth was cruel and cavernous.
The bear said, Isabel, glad to meet you,
How do, Isabel, now I'll eat you!
Isabel, Isabel, didn't worry.
Isabel didn't scream or scurry.
She washed her hands and she straightened her hair up,
Then Isabel quietly ate the bear up.

2 Once in a night as black as pitch
Isabel met a wicked witch.
The witch's face was cross and wrinkled,
The witch's gums with teeth were sprinkled.
Ho, ho, Isabel! the old witch crowed,
I'll turn you into an ugly toad!
Isabel, Isabel, didn't worry,
Isabel didn't scream or scurry,
She showed no rage and she showed nc rancour,
But she turned the witch into milk and drank her.

3 Isabel met a hideous giant,
Isabel continued self-reliant.
The giant was hairy, the giant was horrid,
He had one eye in the middle of his forehead.
Good morning, Isabel, the giant said,
I'll grind your bones to make my bread.
Isabel, Isabel, didn't worry,
Isabel didn't scream or scurry.
She nibbled the zwieback that she always fed off,
And when it was gone, she cut the giant's head off.

4 Isabel met a troublesome doctor,
He punched and he poked till he really shocked her.
The doctor's talk was of coughs and chills
And the doctor's satchel bulged with pills.
The doctor said unto Isabel,
Swallow this, it will make you well.
Isabel, Isabel, didn't worry,
Isabel didn't scream or scurry.
She took those pills from the pill concocter,
And Isabel calmly cured the doctor.

Ogden Nash

SCHOLASTIC

What did Isabel do?

▌ In the first stanza the bear was going to eat Isabel, but Isabel ate the bear.

In the second stanza the witch was going to _____.
We think Isabel will _____,
because _____.

In the third stanza the giant was going to _____.
We think Isabel will _____,
because _____.

In the fourth stanza the doctor was going to _____.
We think Isabel will _____,
because _____.

▌ Use your ideas about what you think Isabel did to write the final line of each stanza of the poem. Remember that the last two lines rhyme with each other.

First stanza

She washed her hands and she straightened her hair up,
Then Isabel quietly ate the bear up.

Second stanza

She showed no rage and she showed no rancour,

_____

Third stanza

She nibbled the zwieback that she always fed off,

_____

Fourth stanza

She took those pills from the pill concocter,

_____